101
SPECIAL TEAMS
DRILLS

Paul McCord

ISBN:1-58518-592-2
Library of Congress Catalog Card Number: 2001098592

Book design and diagrams: Jeanne Hamilton
Cover design: Rebecca Gold Rubin
Front cover photo: Phil Hoffman

Coaches Choice
P.O. Box 1828
Monterey, CA 93942
www.coacheschoice.com

DEDICATION

To my mother and father, Joanne and Jim, without whose love and support I could not have pursued my football careers. For Mindy, thank you for showing me what Christian friendship is all about and for holding me accountable.

FOREWORD

Every coach will tell you that special teams are one-third of the game. Show me a coach who truly believes and implements that concept and I will show you a winning coach. Coach McCord worked with us during our 2000 Super Bowl year and has an excellent grasp of this all-important aspect of the game. In his book *101 Special Teams Drills*, he gives you an excellent outline of important and meaningful perspectives on preparing your team to play effectively on special teams. This book is one that every coach should make a part of his coaching library.

Brian Billick
Head Coach
Baltimore Ravens

ACKNOWLEDGMENTS

I have been blessed by witnessing great leadership in coaching. I would like to thank Brian Billick, Russ Purnell and the entire Baltimore Raven "Super" family for allowing me the privilege to be a part of a fantastic World Championship journey. Thanks to all my special teams warriors at Western Maryland College, you were the embodiment of "Terror" on the field and class off the field. Thank you to Gene Muriaty, Dick Pierce, Sean Landetta and Bob Baker for your teachings and enthusiasm for young specialists. I also owe a debt of gratitude to Tom Lapinski, a true example of a 'teaching coach' in every way. Finally, with personal appreciation to Joe Gardi, head football coach at Hofstra, for all that he has done throughout his career for special teams and for all that he has done for me as a mentor.

CONTENTS

INTRODUCTION

As have many coaches, I have been fortunate to study under some fantastic special teams coaches. All have held the title "guru" at one time or another. Much of what you read in this book is my notes from some of the best names in high school, college and professional coaching. Some drills are mergers of two drills, or adaptations from offensive or defensive drills. A few drills were created on the fly while trying to teach a particular aspect of special teams play. I feel this is where the modern special teams game is heading. There are a few pioneers out there who have taken the basic sound principles of the kicking game and added an explosive element through preparation, opponent scouting and creativity. These pioneers certainly have taken the road less traveled to get to their respective positions. It is my hope that this book brings you the spirit of the creative drives of these pioneer special teams coaches and puts it in easy to understand terms for you and your special teams staff.

If you are a special teams coach, good luck! I am sure that there are several drills you will find in this book to fill your practice schedule and provide your team with good preparation. Remember, the creative element of special teams and modify or advance these drills to suit your needs and your system. Whereas offense and defense have been continually evolving for over 100 years, change in the way that teams approach their special teams has been gradual. Today, successful teams are buying into the fact that field position can be established with a great kicking game...not just a 'safe and sound' kicking game, but an attacking, dynamic kicking game with players who diligently prepare each week for the 25 potentially game-breaking plays in which special teams are involved — and a chance for future stars to shine and veteran players to selflessly lead.

If you are not a special teams coach, but have an added duty in your job description, such as 'punt coach' or 'kickoff coach', these drills will help you understand and organize your specialty. Who knows, you may like coaching special teams so much that you evolve into a special teams junky and coordinator! This book holds helpful information for both the junkie and the coach who is just looking for a quick special teams fix to get him through the season. Whatever your purpose and focus, best of luck and "Good Special Teams!"

PART I

PREPARING TO PLAY

The drills in Chapter 1 are designed to prepare a player's joints for the sudden impacts and quick changes of direction that are necessary for successful special teams play. Studies show that a dynamic, proper warm-up can help prevent injuries. The following drills combine advanced warm-up principles with key elements in covering and blocking skills in the open field. In addition, several speed-development drills have been included in this section. Speed is a particularly key trait for those players who make a living operating in the open field. These dynamic warm-up drills can be performed at multiple speeds with a dual emphasis placed on biomechanical skills and muscle-coordination development.

Getting Ready to Play

An entire team can be warmed up using these drills, but the special teams application of these drills is the key to their effectiveness. These drills should especially benefit the younger players in any program. Even an NFL rookie who is not accustomed to special teams play in college can reacclimate his body to the open-field coverage and blocking techniques attendant to basic special teams principles by using these drills. While practice time for special teams can be limited in the number of actual repetitions accorded special teams in practice, these warm-up drills provide a team with "hidden time" to practice body positioning and technique when there is little practice time to do so. Bear in mind, special teams play is much different on the body than other facets of the game. Moving side-to-side from a full sprint is unique, as are the blocking acquisitions in the open field. You and your staff can use these warm-ups for your entire team while your special teams players develop at much faster rates and get some "individual" time during practice.

CHAPTER 1

WARM-UP
DRILLS

Drill #1: COVER AND RECOVER DRILL

Objective: To warm-up; improve change of direction ability; acclimate athletes to playing surface; teach proper balance position in blocking and tackling in the open field.

Equipment Needed: A lined field.

Description: The coach stands in the front of five groups of players. The facing players should be approximately five yards apart and be in balanced stances with one foot in front of the other (i.e., wide-receiver stances). Players should be ready to roll forward on the command of the coach. The players are given a direction to begin their run – right, left or straight. On the coach's command, the players roll forward and run in the direction instructed by the coach. At 15 yards, players are to come to a balanced position, with their head and eyes up and shuffle sideways in the direction of the coach's command. The coach should command "break right" or "break left" and should either point or jog in that direction. After the players reach the sideline, they should return to their lines for another rep. The drill should be run until each player has stemmed each direction (R,L,M) and broken to both command sides (R, L). The warm-up pace should be controlled, but rigorous. This drill can be done at full speed if used in the middle of practice.

Coaching Points:

- When covering the field, the player's eyes should be up, and the players should be prepared to react to a visual cue.

- The coach should emphasize the need to make a change of direction from a balanced, controlled position.

- The team element in tackling by developing your players' sense of peripheral vision and side awareness in coverage should be stressed. Each player should ask himself, "Who's next to me?"

"Angle left" Command

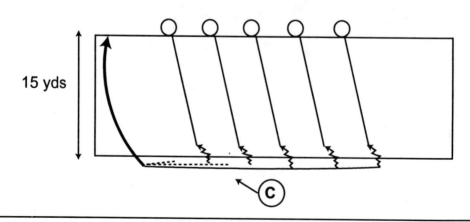

15 yds

Drill #2: DROP STEP SLIDE DRILL

Objective: To warm-up; loosen up the hips of players; work proper open-field body positioning.

Equipment Needed: A lined field, or cones.

Description: This drill goes across the width of the field. It is a simplistic approach to loosening the hips of players prior to performing a full-speed drill. In basketball, it is a variation of the "drop-step" drill. Simply get two to four lines of players on yard lines five yards apart. The players begin by facing the coach. The coach points to a direction and commands, "Drop and slide!" Players should open their hip at a 45-degree angle and quickly slide to the direction's side with their eyes on the coach. When a player touches the line to the direction side with his call-side foot, he should open and rotate his hips, quickly and smoothly, toward his origin line and shuffle back (90-degrees). The drill is intended to go from 15-25 yards in length as a warm-up. Players need to stay in a good, low balanced position and reach with their slide-side foot to gain maximum ground, while quickly shuffling their feet for maximum quickness. This drill can be used as a conditioner if the distance is more than 25-yards per repetition.

Coaching Points:

- Players should stay low in their stance – the low man wins.

- The coach should require discipline in the players in maintaining proper form with their feet, thereby enhancing their level of control and coordination.

- Players should keep their eyes forward and their heads up.

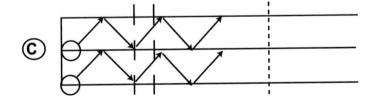

Drill #3: EXPLOSIVE ROPE RELEASE DRILL

Objective: To warm-up; enhance explosiveness; encourage good running form; improve running strength and knee lift.

Equipment Needed: One rope for each group and two nylon belts with industrial loops (or any belt with a moveable loop); a lined field or a measured track.

Description: Have players partner up with someone of similar size. Each player puts on a belt securely with the washer or loop moved to the player's rear. The player (A) designated to go first gets into a 3-point, mountain-climber stance and gets ready to run. The partner (B) slips the rope through the loop and wraps his left hand in the rope, while his right hand grasps the rope and he holds the rope in his palm. On player B's command, player A stays low and controlled out of his stance and sprints with high-knee lift for 10 yards. Player B should hold the rope, but enable player A to run at 80% of his fastest speed – in other words, player A should be able to run smoothly, and should not be resisted too much. At the 10-yard line, player B lets go of the rope in his right palm. Player A explodes forward and works to maintain his new speed for 30 yards before decelerating under control and jogging back to the line. The distances of resistance and sprinting can be manipulated. The total time elapsed for the drill should be no more than 15 seconds from start to deceleration.

Coaching Points:

- Players should run in a relaxed manner and maintain symmetry in their form. Coaches should look at facial expressions and ease of motor movement to gage player form. Athletes should be encouraged to maintain strong knee raises in their form to promote running power.

- The amount of resistance is crucial! Players should run out of their stances without TOO MUCH resistance. Too much resistance promotes a power drill, more suited to offensive and defensive line play than speed development.

- This is a good finishing warm-up since it requires a more complex order of movement and more fatigue factors in the muscle groups. This drill could be used as a conditioner as well, but the athletes should be given adequate recovery time between sprint.

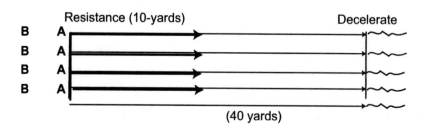

Drill #4: LATERAL ROPE RELEASE DRILL

Objective: To warm-up; increase lateral explosiveness and speed; increase coordination from a proper special teams position.

Equipment Needed: One rope for each group and two nylon belts with industrial loops (or any belt with a moveable loop); a lined field or a measured track.

Description: Have players partner up with someone of similar size. Each player puts on a belt securely with the washer or loop moved to the player's side (left or right.) The player (A) designated to go first gets into a balanced stance facing the coach and gets ready to slide. The partner (B) slips the rope through the loop and wraps his left hand in the rope, while his right hand grasps the rope and he holds the rope in his palm. On player B's command, player A stays low and either shuffles <u>or</u> carriokas away from player B. Player B allows A to slide at 80% his normal speed and releases A at 10 yards by letting go of the rope in his right hand. Player A slides an additional 10 yards from the release point, keeping his head and eyes up and moving quickly. After 10 yards, player A turns his hips and jogs 10 yards to decelerate. The distances of resistance and sprinting can be manipulated. The total time elapsed for the drill should be no more than 15 seconds from start to deceleration.

Coaching Points:

- The amount of resistance is crucial! Players should run out of their stances without TOO MUCH resistance. Too much resistance promotes a power drill, more suited to offensive and defensive line play than speed development.

- A quick, reaching step and fast foot recovery should be emphasized. Players should use their arms to enable increased propulsion laterally. "Sliding on hot coals" is a good analogy to picture.

- The swiveling of the hips upon deceleration is an important part of this drill. Finish!!!

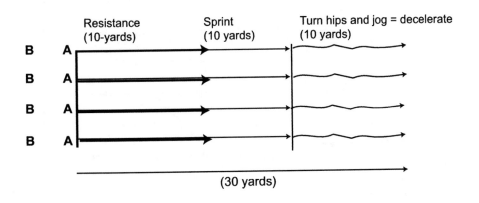

Drill #5: SPRINT, ANGLE, RECOVER DRILL

Objective: To warm-up; improve change of direction ability; acclimate each player to the playing surface; work explosiveness at various body angles and positions.

Equipment Needed: A lined field.

Description: This is a jogging drill that focuses on the explosive change-of-direction movements made when reacting to plays in the open field. Players get into evenly distributed lines on the sideline at a yard line five yards apart (Note: The accompanying diagram shows players who are 10 yards apart for better clarity.) The first player in line begins on the command or whistle of the coach. The player jogs out on the line and on his fifth step plants on his outside foot and explodes at a 45-degree angle to the opposite yard line. Upon reaching the opposite yard line, the player plants his outside foot and turns 90-degrees and jogs to the line of origin. When reaching the line of origin, the player plants his outside foot and turns 90-degrees to the original jog position. The player repeats the drill from the other side of field, working opposite turns.

Coaching Points:

- The players should keep their head and eyes forward at all times. Emphasize their ability to see other players in the drill with their peripheral vision, but not to have to turn to locate them.

- The players need to accelerate under control in their cuts. This is done by keep a low center of gravity and using their arms and hands to aid their lower body balance.

- The focus of the drill should be on the quickness of the players coming into and out of their open-field cuts, rather than straight-ahead sprint speed.

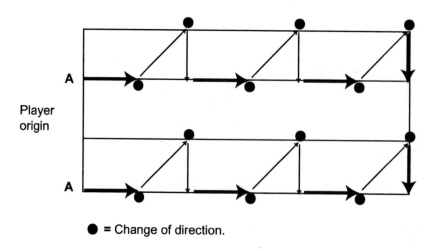

● = Change of direction.

Drill #6: MULTIPLE RUNNING SKILLS DRILL

Objective: To warm-up; loosen up a player's hips; develop body coordination; quicken feet.

Equipment Needed: A lined field with landmarks (i.e., numbers, hash marks).

Description: Using any combination of form-running drills, this drill challenges a player's coordination and quickness simultaneously. Players divide into evenly distributed groups on the sideline, looking across a yard line. The coach tells the players they are to do two different, predetermined agilities and to alternate each agility on each landmark (numbers, hash) across the field. On command, the players begin working across the field, remaining on their line. The drill is completed when the athlete has crossed the field. After one length of the field, the coach can change the agilities.

Coaching Points:

- A coach can choose from any of the following agilities and put in any order or combination: high knee, high-knee crossover, fast feet, carrioka (quick or long strides), slide shuffle, bounding (alternate, or single leg), skip hops, and back-pedal.

- The players should maintain their focus on making smooth, controlled transitions and to using their arms to aid propulsion across the field.

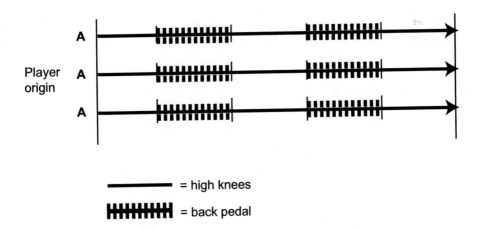

Drill #7: TEAM REACTION DRILL

Objective: To warm-up; work balance skills as a team; promote quick reactions; loosen the hips; work on foot agility.

Equipment Needed: A football.

Description: Have a captain, or coach, face the players. Players are grouped in lines five yards apart from the nearest line and spaced five yards front and back. The leader starts the drill with a "set" command. All players should be in a balanced stance with their feet slightly greater than shoulder width apart and their hands relaxed in front of their torso. The drill leader (DL) will pause and begin one of five different movements that must be mimicked or reacted to by the team. The DL turns and jogs right/left – the team then shuffles right/left. The DL hits the ground and explodes up; the team then hits the ground and explodes up. The DL moves forward; the team then drop steps and shuffles, keeping the DL to their inside perspective. The DL back pedals while the team slides forward keeping the DL on their inside shoulder. The DL chops his feet, and the team chops their feet vigorously. If the DL says, "BALL!!", the players rush the DL. The first player in wraps the DL while the next players corral the DL with their heads and eyes up.

Coaching Points:

- A coach can modify the drill to fit different agilities — stress what he wants to emphasize.

- A coach should make sure that his players are enthusiastic as a team — "Eleven sets of eyes are one!"

- All players should work on their reaction times and foot coordination, while being sensitive to the need for maintaining proper posture and body positioning.

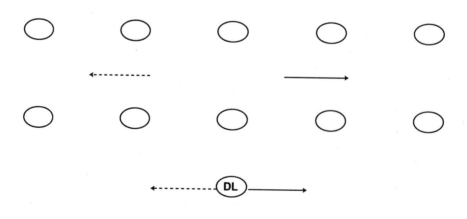

Drill #8: HURDLE SQUARE DRILL

Objective: To warm up; promote hip flexibility and muscle control; stretch leg muscles.

Equipment Needed: Four cones.

Description: Space the cones in a 5-yard square and align one line of players behind one of the cones, facing directly across from another cone on the outside of the box. This is a sequential drill. When a player reaches the first cone, the next player in line follows. With his hands on his hips for balance, the first player begins a front-hurdle rotation walk towards the first cone. Walking his left leg forward, the player rotates his right leg slowly forward, as if rolling over a hurdle. When his right foot hits the ground as part of the natural movement of the leg, the player should roll onto the ball of his right foot and work his left leg over the pretend hurdle. This is not a rushed drill. The objective is for coordinated movement and a smooth transition from leg-to-leg. When reaching the first cone, the player slide shuffles slowly his left to the next cone and walks backward with an external hip rotation. The player will drive his first knee up toward his chest, and then rotate his leg outside and extend backward and onto his toe. The player repeats with his opposite leg, and continues backward walking until reaching the final cone. The drill continues until each person has gone through the box. To work both sides, the players will execute the drill from the opposite side after they have all gone through one way.

Coaching Points:

- Uncoordinated athletes in particular need to focus on this drill. In fact, however, the attention to body movement and increased hip flexibility is an excellent primer for the joints of any player who is engaged in a lot of changes of direction. Be strict with all your player's movements.

- Players should rotate their legs at the highest angles possible. When going over the imaginary hurdle, their entire leg should be parallel to the ground.

- Players should be prevented from bouncing with their plant leg to facilitate the movement of their hurdle legs. Remind athletes who are somewhat lacking in coordination that doing the drill properly will enable them to acquire greater hip flexibility over time.

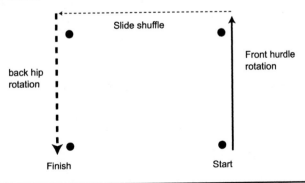

Drill #9: GET OFF YOUR FACE DRILL

Objective: To increase leg turnover and speed; train eyes to visual cues; emphasize recovering in coverage; warm-up.

Equipment Needed: A lined field.

Description: The players form equal lines evenly spaced apart across a yard line. The coach stands 20 yards away, facing the players. The players in the front of the line get into a push-up position with their chests on the ground and their head and eyes on the coach. The coach then says, "Get Up!" at which time the players push off their hands as they cycle their feet underneath their bodies and accelerate twenty yards before slowing down. The drill should be done until each player has gone down and back. Since everyone gets knocked down at some point on special teams, this drill enables players to enhance their ability (and their sense of pride) to get up and get after "it."

Coaching Points:

- The coach can hold the players in a push-up position and vary how long the players are on the ground. Doing so will require the players to focus their eyes for a longer period of time and prevent them from getting an unrealistic jump on the call.

- It should be stressed to the players to get their legs under them and to move as quickly as possible. Some players will try to reach and stride off the ground and, as a result, will lag behind.

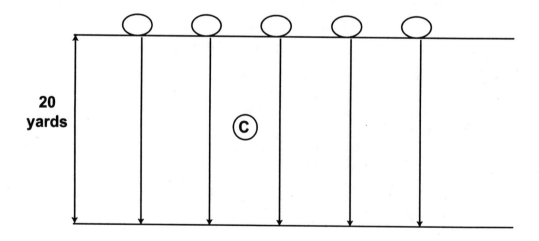

Drill #10: DODGE & WEAVE DRILL

Objective: Loosen up the hips of players; warm-up; teach coordination and body control in the open field.

Equipment Needed: None.

Description: The players get into two lines spread down the field 5-yards apart from each other. The first player assumes a 2-point, receiver's stance and rolls forward on command, running at the number of the first player facing him. As the player approaches the first player in line, he wiggles his body to one shoulder, avoiding contact narrowly while staying on course to the next player in line. The player should gradually reach top speed as he weaves around the first stationary player and runs to the opposite side of the next stationary player. The sequence is then repeated, somewhat like a slalom course, until the player sprints 10 yards past the final object. The first player to run then assumes the final position in the course, and the drill moves continuously down the field until all of the players have taken part in the drill, or the field is used. In the latter instance, the coach may choose to return the length of the field to finish the drill.

Coaching Points:

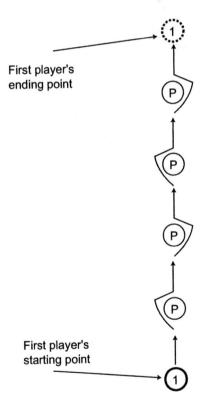

First player's ending point

First player's starting point

- The players need to run directly at the target before dodging to one side of him. Good body lean and control should be emphasized.

- Although players are dodging, they need to run through the course without stopping their feet or making a plant cut. Going through this drill at half-speed and gradually picking up time should help players be more aware of their body lean as they reach their faster speed.

- Each line of players should be grouped by comparable speed so players are not on top of each other as they run. Having a player count to three before peeling into the drill can also help with spacing.

PART II

SPECIALIST
DRILLS

CHAPTER 2

DRILLS FOR PUNTERS

Drill #11: DYNAMIC LEG SWINGS DRILL

Objective: To dynamically warm-up a punter; increase flexibility and leg speed.

Equipment Needed: A fence, goal post, bleacher, balance mount (found in dance rooms), or a sturdy stationary object.

Description: The punter should stand and face a suspended stationary object, such as a fence, and securely grasp it with both hands. The punter should extend his arms away from the fence, providing room for the exercise. While keeping his torso as erect as possible, the punter should swing his leg outside in, and then inside out, gradually building height on the pendulum swings. He should repeat the swings at least 10 times, exhaling as his leg rotates out to help relax his inner thigh, hamstring and groin. The punter should then repeat this dynamic leg swing with his opposite leg. After working the side rotation of his leg, the punter should then turn parallel to the fence, grasping it with the hand closest to it. While standing on his outside leg, the punter should now swing his leg in a pendulum motion front-to-back, like his punting motion, building gradually to full extension, but keeping continuous motion in the leg swing. As the punter's leg swings behind him, the punter should visualize a relaxed sweeping motion and try to extend his leg as far back as possible, with very little bending of the knee. Each leg should execute 10 full leg swings, with emphasis placed on the punter breathing out on the upward front swing of the leg.

Coaching Points:

- Each punter should pay particular attention to his level of flexibility. Proper breathing techniques have been shown to relax major muscle groups, thereby increasing flexibility.

- Working different angles of the leg swing will promote an enhanced level of flexibility of different muscle groups.

- The punters should be kept under control when doing any drill. They must learn to focus on minute details in their stretches. This attention to detail can carry over to the teaching of minute details in their punting techniques.

Drill #12: BAD SNAP DRILL

Objective: To develop and improve the punter's use of hands and footwork; prepare punters for handling pressure situations in a routine manner; develop hand-eye coordination and focus.

Equipment Needed: A football.

Description: In this drill, the coach stands at the regular distance from the snapper to the punter that his team uses. The coach either snaps or simulates a snap to the punter. The snap must be fieldable, but can be anywhere within the punter's range. The punter should catch the ball and simulate his steps while putting the ball in proper drop position as quickly as possible. After successfully fielding a variety of bad snaps, the punter can then begin making contact with the ball. It is important to have the punter work at fielding the ball in all conceivable directions.

Coaching Points:

- Bad snaps can be thrown in a variety of places in order to challenge the punter to slide his feet from side-to-side while remaining square to the LOS. Keeping in front of the ball is the primary key to handling a bad snap.

- The punter's ball positioning after catching/fielding a poor snap should be observed. If he has trouble getting a good handle on the ball, do not add the element of punting. The punter should work hard to develop his hands with other hands drills that are included in this book.

- The coach can slow down the drill and describe specific scenarios that the punter may face during a game so he can practice what to do in all eventualities. If he can't handle the poor snap, the coach should go over what he wants his punter to do.

- One possible variation for this drill is to use a "heavy ball" if your punter has outstanding hands. This step can make his hands even better because a heavy ball adds to the difficulty of making a clean catch and holding the ball properly. Note: THE PUNTER SHOULD <u>NOT</u> PUNT A HEAVY BALL.

Drill #13: ROTATING LACES DRILL

Objective: To develop sure-handed punters; to increase hand-eye coordination and focus; prevent leg fatigue that can result from "over-punting."

Equipment Needed: A football.

Description: The punter should stand a yard from the coach who holds the ball behind his back. The coach holds the ball, with the laces in the palm of his hand. Coach says "set" and underhands the ball to the punter who brings his hands up and simulates a catch. Upon receiving the ball, the punter manipulates the laces to get them on top, in the position he feels most comfortable with, and in his drop position away from his body. While this motion should be smooth and quick, his arms and hands must not be clinched or tight. The punter then quickly hands the ball back to the coach who reorients the ball to a random position behind his back before calling "set" again and rapidly underhanding the ball back to the punter. This drill can continue for as long as the coach and punter want to work. The coach can count how many perfect drop positions are achieved in an elapsed period of time to add an element of pressure and competition to the drill.

Coaching Points:

- The coach can hide the ball from the punter and not allow him to have any clue where the laces will be in order to simulate a game the best way possible.

- The punter should be in a good, balanced stance with his weight well distributed. The same stance the punter will employ in a game should be used in this drill.

- When the punter makes a mistake, the coach should review with him what went wrong. Often times, a punter will have problems with one particular receiving position. If that position can be identified and worked on in this drill, this drill can help the punter solve his problem.

Drill #14: STEPPING DOWN THE TARGET LINE DRILL

Objective: To improve the footwork of the punter; reinforce the linear principles involved in punting; improve mental imagery; improve focus and control.

Equipment Needed: A lined field; a football.

Description: The player straddles a yard line and looks across the field. His kicking foot should be bordering one edge of a standard yard line, and his non-kicking foot should be on the other side of the line, wherever it naturally falls in his stance. The punter begins the drill by visualizing a snap and receiving the 'ball'. The punter executes his punt without the ball and attempts to keep his body straight and his feet parallel, but not crossing over each other. His plant foot should be on the line as his leg begins to swing, but not in front of his kicking foot's original placement position. The punter swings through the punt with a normal follow-through, while over exaggerating his focus down on the ball (i.e., keeping his head down). The punter executes this drill across the field and back, moving forward with each mock punt attempt. To make the drill more advanced, the coach can then add a ball that the punter kicks out of his hand (i.e., no snap). The coach should have the punter swing through his punts while focusing PRIMARILY on the drill and not the result! The punter should stay in one particular part of the field and punt across the yard line. The coach can also add a snap to the drill once the first two parts of this drill are done well. The snaps should simulate game conditions as much as possible.

Coaching Points:

- The coaching focus should be kept on the punter's feet, not where the ball goes. Use your ears and listen for good contact.

- The punter should be encouraged to straddle the line – never to cross over with either foot. If the punter chronically crosses over, one possible option is to ask him to think about walking bowlegged during each approach.

- The first part of this drill can be used as a warm-up or a conditioning exercise. It could give the punter something to do that won't tire his leg as the season progresses.

Drill #15: THE DROP DRILL

Objective: To improve the consistency of a punter's drop; increase concentration levels; improve awareness of punting mechanics; provide the punter with a non-physically taxing drill.

Equipment Needed: A football.

Description: In this drill, the ball is not punted, and there is no leg swing. The drill begins with the ball in the punter's hands. After simulating receiving the snap by spinning the ball in his hands, the punter then begins his natural stepping pattern. When the punter gets to his drop release, he should follow the ball with his eyes, but stop the rest of his punting motion. On an ideal drop, the ball will fall to the ground and bounce straight up. The punter should focus his energy on creating the perfect drop, while focusing on the 'sweet spot' on the ball with his eyes. Most punters do not focus on anything in particular when they drop the football. This approach creates greater variety of impact area since no visual 'target' is selected. It would be like shooting target practice and not locating the bullseye before the shot. After the punter has mastered this drill, the coach can provide a snap and increase the level of realism. This additional step would enable the punter to also work on his ball-handling skills.

Coaching Points:

- The punter should have his drop arm fully extended. This positioning will enable the ball to travel away from his body and in turn allow his leg to reach full extension on the punt.

- The coach should find the laces of the punt. If he is standing in front of the punter, the position of the laces should be straight, or only slightly angled in (less than 10 degrees). The greater the angle, the better the chance of poor leg swing (across punter's body).

- A game environment should be created as much as possible. The punter should get used to working his drop under pressure. In games, the most costly mistake a punter can make is a poor drop.

Drill #16: THE PULL DRILL

Objective: To increase drop consistency; improve stepping pattern; improve body mechanics and awareness; provide an exercise that is non-taxing on punter's legs.

Equipment Needed: A football.

Description: The coach stands facing the punter about four yards away, favoring the punter's foot side. Holding the ball by the laces, the coach simulates a snap to the punter and slides to the punter's leg side, allowing the punter room to perform the drill. The punter catches the ball and steps straight ahead using his normal stepping and drop pattern. When the ball is dropped, the coach quickly pulls the ball away from the punter, allowing the punter to swing through on air. The drill is repeated until the punter has traveled a pre-determined distance (on average, 50 yards). The drill resets after each rep and gradually works down the field. This drill can be combined with the "stepping down your target line" drill (Drill #14) to provide the punter with a visual target stepping line if his stepping pattern is erratic.

Coaching Points:

- Immediate feedback should be provided to the punter on each rep. The punter should be told where his drop positioning was in relationship to his body. Make sure the ball travels far enough to get onto the hitting surface of the foot.

- The drop angle and trajectory of the ball should be analyzed, while examining the punter's leg swing. A straight and effortless leg extension is key to successful punting.

- The coach should create game conditions and pressure, while encouraging the punter to remain relaxed.

Drill #17: NO-STEP PUNTING DRILL

Objective: To improve the punter's balance, coordination and concentration; develop a feel for the proper hitting surface on the foot; ensure proper leg swing and follow-through.

Equipment Needed: A football or a bag of footballs.

Description: This drill may feel very awkward to young punters. The punter assumes the same extended position he takes in his regular technique on his last step. To ensure proper body alignment, the punter should go through a punt and "freeze frame" immediately prior to his drop. The punter's plant foot should be on the ground with his drop arm and elbow fully extended away from his body. His non-drop arm should be even with his chest, off of the ball. In this awkward position, the punter should drop the ball and swing through the punt as he would with a normal punt. His hips should finish through the punt and remain square to the target. Punters should not be as worried about the resulting punt as they are over their drop technique and follow-through, but eventually they should be able to control the punt's direction and quality.

Coaching Points:

- The punter should be encouraged to feel the drop hitting his foot. Punters need to develop the 'memory' of where the ball needs to hit their foot on good punts. This technique will lead to them to better understand and appreciate the proper biomechanics of the movement. Ideally, the ball should hit in the middle of the foot, but it may feel to the punter like the middle and outside of his foot are both being hit simultaneously. This feeling occurs because when the punt has been hit well, the ball has been hit with maximum surface area on the foot.

- The coach should observe the punter's body control and work to keep him square through his kick. In addition, the punter's off arm should be checked to make sure it is under control. (Note: The opposite arm can be used as a balance in front of his body on the follow-through.)

Drill #18: ONE-STEP PUNTING DRILL

Objective: To improve a punter's balance, coordination and concentration; develop a feel for the proper hitting surface on the foot; ensure proper leg swing and follow-through; provide an alternative drill to the no-step for younger punters.

Equipment Needed: A football or a bag of footballs.

Description: This drill may either accompany the no-step drill or be used as an alternative exercise for younger punters who do not have the body coordination to complete the no-step drill successfully. To ensure the proper body alignment, the punter (2-step punter) should execute his steps and "freeze frame" after his first step. Both of his hands should still be on the ball, or his off hand should be just coming off the ball, but in front of his body. His drop arm and elbow should be fully extended. He should maintain a good posture, while standing with his weight primarily on his punting foot. The punter should roll forward and execute a punt from the one-step position. To increase the level of difficulty of the drill, the coach can snap the ball to the punter who should quickly orient the ball to the ideal drop position, and then execute the one-step punt.

Coaching Points:

- The coach should check the punter for out-of-control body parts and ensure that the punter's opposite arm is aiding the follow-through and not pulling his shoulder away from the leg swing. His shoulders and hips should be square to the target at all times.

- The punter should be encouraged to feel the drop hitting his foot. Punters need to develop the 'memory' of where the ball should to hit their foot on good punts. Ideally, the ball should hit in the middle of the punter's foot, although it may feel to him like the middle and outside of his foot are both being hit simultaneously. This feeling occurs because when a punt has been hit well, the ball has been hit with maximum surface area on the foot.

- The punter should employ this drill to help improve his quickness. He should have a quick tempo once he masters the mechanics of the drill. This technique will improve the punter's speed and get away times.

Drill #19: TAPS DRILL

Objective: To develop a feel for the proper hitting surface on the foot; ensure proper leg swing and follow-through; dynamically loosen up or cool down the leg.

Equipment Needed: A football.

Description: The coach and player get 10 yards apart, facing each other. Taking a step, the punter holds the ball out and swings his leg, tapping it to the coach. The player can achieve a spiral on the ball by tapping the proper hitting surface of his foot and extending his drop away from his body. The drill continues at 10 yards until three good taps are made. Then, the coach and player back up five yards each. The punter should strive for accuracy in his taps to the coach. The height of the punt should start low, and gradually build, never becoming the focus of the drill. The punter and coach continue the drill through 30 yards, or until each is satisfied with the progress of the drill.

Coaching Points:

* The coach should play catch with his punter. The punter needs to be as accurate punting the ball as the coach is at throwing it back to him.

* A low drop to the punter should be stressed. The punter should be encouraged to develop a quick, pendulum-leg swing. Quickly sweeping the leg with a low drop minimizes the "float time" of the drop, which in turn decreases the effect of wind on the drop's trajectory. In other words, the less "float time" in a windy area, the more consistent the drop and punt.

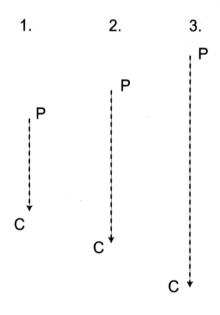

Drill #20: LINE DRIVE DRILL

Objective: To increase drop consistency; improve leg speed and trajectory; improve hand-eye coordination.

Equipment Needed: A football or a bag of footballs.

Description: The objective of this drill is to drive punts at low angles, like passes, to a partner or partners. Punters should space themselves 30-50 yards apart from each other, depending on their leg strength and ability. Each punter should be the same distance apart from the other punters (i.e., equidistant). The drill begins with the punter who is holding the ball line-driving a punt directly to another punter. The punters should lower their drops and work a quick, sweeping leg swing with their toes completely depressed to get best results. Punters compete against each other to determine who is the most accurate punter and who hits the tightest spirals. The drill can be performed for either a timed period, or until each punter has achieved maximum results for a certain number of reps.

Coaching Points:

- Punters should follow-through properly and not come across their bodies. This action is called 'cutting' or 'slicing' the ball and can lead to erratic punts when the pressure is on!

- Punters need to maintain a quick pendulum swing to get up and through the ball.

- It should be emphasized to punters that they should maintain a good follow-through position with their head and their eyes focused on the ball downward. They should exaggerate this positioning in their follow-through to prevent them from picking their heads up early.

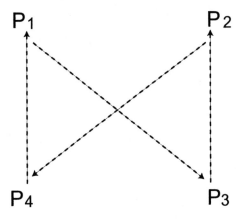

Punters 40-yards apart

Drill #21: GAUNTLET PUNTING DRILL

Objective: To improve directional punting; reinforce the linear principles involved in punting; enhance coordination and body control.

Equipment Needed: Ten small cones; a football or a bag of footballs.

Description: Six cones are assembled in a gauntlet one yard apart and four yards long from the 25 to the 29-yard line. The cones should be across from one another, positioned in a gauntlet involving three pairs of cones. On the opposite 25-yard line, the remaining cones are positioned in a 5-yard box that reaches the 20-yard line. The punter assumes his normal stance as if he were punting straight down field. The coach snaps the ball to the punter. The punter must stay within the gauntlet during the entire movement of the punt. On his follow-through, the coach should be able to see if the punter's leg swing and hips remained square during the punt. The punter wants to drop as many balls as possible with consistent hang times into the box downfield (40-45 yards). The drill can be made directional by angling the gauntlet and downfield box right or left. The coach could require the punter to perform a set of five punts each direction and force him to operate from within the gauntlet.

Coaching Points:

- The punter should be reminded that he should stay in the gauntlet at all times. The cones should be untouched, and the punter's follow-through should not break the plane of either cone at the end of the gauntlet.

- If the punter has a good stepping pattern and stays square, his drop will be responsible for any deviation in the accuracy of his punt.

- This drill works well with punters who chronically swing across their bodies, or step crooked on their approach.

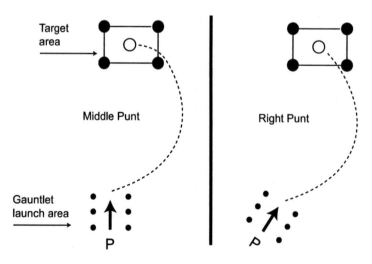

Drill #22: PRESSURE PUNT DRILL

Objective: To pressure the punter in a safe environment; improve focus; decrease get away-times; provide variety in a punting workout.

Equipment Needed: A football or a bag of footballs.

Description: In this drill, the coach, or group of players, applies visual and verbal pressure on the punter. With a long snapper, two players align facing the punter on the other side of the LOS. On the snap of the ball, the players rush the punter on either side, keeping a yard of space to both sides of him. As the punter drops the ball, the players should be yelling or attempting to distract the punter from his task. If the coach does not have players he trusts to stay off the punter, he could have two players stand on either side of the punter and walk along side of him as he punts the ball. These two players could distract the punter without touching him. If the coach is alone with the punter, he can snap the ball underhand, and then rush to one side or another, creating a distraction.

Coaching Points:

- People should be kept away from the punter as he punts the ball. Have the players find ingenious ways to distract the attention of the punter.

- The punter needs to focus on small things when he is in a pressure situation. He should concentrate on his sweet spot (i.e., the focus point on the ball).

- If the punter pops his head up early in the punt, he should be reminded to exaggerate his head downward on his follow-through.

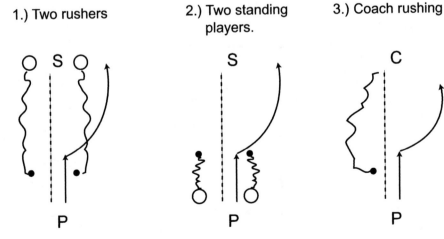

1.) Two rushers   2.) Two standing players.   3.) Coach rushing

Drill #23: EXTENSION DRILL

Objective: To improve leg extension and flexibility; develop hang time; reinforce linear concepts of punting.

Equipment Needed: A goal post; a bag of footballs.

Description: Depending on the size and step length of the punter, an origin point should be marked that would enable the punter to make ball/foot contact exactly three yards from the crossbar (10-feet tall). The coach should stand at the end line of the field underneath the cross bar and underhand snap the ball to the punter. The punter should then punt the ball, ensuring that the ball clears the crossbar, while he remains square to his target. The punter should feel his foot rising over the crossbar (from his perspective) and visualize a high punt. His leg should be fully extended. The drill should be repeated five times. The hang times of each punt should be measured.

Coaching Points:

- The punter's leg extension should be checked and compared to his natural leg swing. If there is a noticeable difference, the punter should do this drill on a regular basis and work on his flexibility.

- The punter should finish square to the coach and the crossbar. This drill emphasizes upward explosion from the hips.

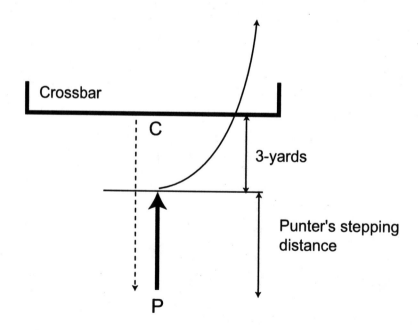

Drill #24: TARGET PRACTICE DRILL

Objective: To improve directional and pooch punting; improve focus and concentration; provide a variety of punts.

Equipment Needed: Ten cones; a bag of footballs.

Description: In this drill, the coach challenges the punter to execute a variety of inside the 50-yard line (i.e., pooch, directional punts) kicks. First, two 10-yard boxes are made using eight of the cones. Next, a cone is placed on the 6-yard line on one college hash and the 8-yard line on the other college hash. The coach tells the punter which punt he should attempt, for example, "pooch punt, 4.5 hang time, inside the 10". The snapper snaps the ball to the punter, and the punter then executes the play. The next punter gets behind the center, and the coach gives him his try. The coach can choose any command he wants. In a normal situation, pooch right, pooch left, pooch middle, coffin corner right/left, or best hang inside the 10 are all viable options. The punters should be rotated through the drill, and the point where their punts land should be charted in relationship to an ideal attempt.

Coaching Points:

- The coach should write down where he wants to focus his attention before he gets on the field. He almost has too many options. Working right, left, middle pooch punting one day would be a good drill, saving coffin corner work for another day. On the other hand, the workout could be scripted and the specialists could be allowed to chart each other sequentially.

- The coach should work to develop the strengths of each individual punter. It is difficult to find a punter that can do all of the essential skills with ease, but most can do one very well. During games, the coach may want to have the security of execution that comes from a punter being superior at one of the skills.

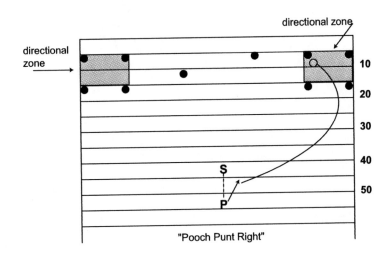

"Pooch Punt Right"

CHAPTER 3

DRILLS FOR KICKERS

Drill #25: KICKS ON AIR DRILL

Objective: To improve visualization skills; increase confidence; dynamically warm-up; improve focus and concentration.

Equipment Needed: A goal post.

Description: The kicker practices lining up and executing perfect kicks, while envisioning pressure situations and a game-like atmosphere. The drill begins with the coach setting up the exact situation in the game and marking the spot of the ball (LOS). The kicker picks his spot, or places his tee, and takes his steps backwards, visualizing his target. After he has reached his walk-off behind his spot, he reacquires his target and takes his steps to the side (conventional kickers will begin focusing on the actual kick procedure at this time). When the steps across have been taken, the kicker again refocuses his eyes on his target before setting into his stance. The kicker visualizes the snap, and then approaches his spot and swings through his kick to full extension. The kicker visualizes his kick going directly to his target. The coach then marks another LOS spot, and the drill continues until the kicker has executed 10 perfect kicks from different spots on the field.

Coaching Points:

- To set up each kick, the coach should prepare the kicker with as many conditions around the kick as possible, (e.g., weather conditions, the opponent, the field or kicking surface, time of game, etc.).

- Great kickers are creatures of habit. They should establish the habit of sighting targets and then visualizing them while focusing on his spot. The coach should make sure everything is done in this drill as it will be done in the game.

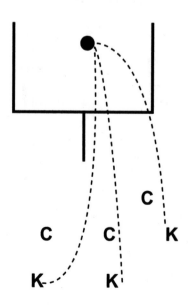

Drill # 26: IMPACT DRILL

Objective: To improve the kicker's understanding of ideal foot/ball contact point; improve balance and concentration; develop sound technique; conserve leg strength.

Equipment Needed: A football.

Description: This drill uses a holder, coach or another kicker to securely hold a football down in front of the kicker. While squarely on both knees, the holder should put downward pressure on the ball, using both hands in front of the ball. His palms should be on the top front panels of the football. The kicker balances himself on his plant foot with his kicking leg off the ground behind the ball. His non-kicking arm should be raised alongside of his body, ready to come forward on the kick. Eyes are positioned low on the back of the ball. On command of the holder, the kicker swings downward on the ball, hitting the sweet spot. The holder provides resistance by giving very slightly to the momentum of the swing. The holder resets the ball, and the kicker then regains his balance and repeats the rep.

Coaching Points:

- Body control and balance should be stressed. This drill is great for helping kickers to become aware of their body positioning on impact with the ball.

- The holder should provide information to the kicker on the foot/ball contact. He will be able to tell how square the impact was and what the trajectory of the kick was. This step will develop more precision and consistency in the contact.

- The kicker's body mechanics should be checked to determine if he is maintaining good habits. His opposite arm should coincide in front of his body as his kicking leg swings. This action serves as a counterbalance to the pendulum swing of the leg.

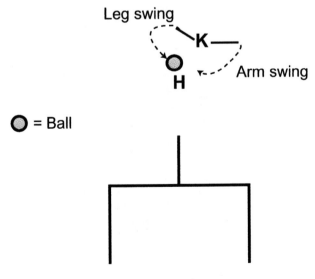

Drill #27: NO-STEP BALANCING KICKS DRILL

Objective: To improve balance and control; emphasize proper foot/ball contact point; develop leg strength; improve kick height and body positioning on follow-through.

Equipment Needed: A bag of footballs.

Description: In this drill, the kicker works on proper impact point and balance. To start the drill, the kicker assumes a pre-kick position, with his plant foot on the ground and his head over top of the ball. The kicker balances himself on his plant foot with his kicking leg off the ground behind the ball. His non-kicking arm should be raised, alongside of his body, ready to come forward on the kick. His eyes are positioned low on the back of the ball. Once the kicker has assumed a balanced position, the holder spots the ball and gives the kicker a number between one and five. The kicker must remain balanced and controlled until the holder completes his count, at which time the kicker should swing through and execute the kick with perfect form.

Coaching Points:

- The ball should be spotted at various angles on the field. The coach should not be concerned if the kicks do not have enough distance. The focus should be on a consistent rotation of the football and a straight-line hit.

- The use of the kicker's entire body in the kick should be emphasized. The kicker's body positioning should be checked after the kick.

- The coach should check for hitches, or jerking movements in the kicker's body and work on the flexibility of those parts of the kicker's body.

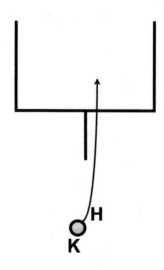

Drill #28: ONE-STEP KICKS DRILL

Objective: To improve balance and control; emphasize proper foot/ball contact point; develop leg accuracy; decrease get-away times.

Equipment Needed: A bag of footballs.

Description: This drill is an abbreviated kicking exercise where the kicker is forced to accurately kick off after taking only one step. To get the proper alignment, the kicker should first align in his normal stepping pattern, and then execute a kick. The coach should attempt to mark, with close proximity, where the position of the kicker's final step is in relation to a straight-ahead, normal kick. The kicker should get his steps for the drill from this position. The drill should initially be performed by having the kicker attempt three kicks from PAT range off of the one-step approach. The holder can either spot the ball to the ground prior to the kicker's steps, or simulate a snap after checking with the kicker. The coach, or holder, can then re-spot the ball anywhere on the field that is within the kicker's range. The kicker should then continue the drill, with an emphasis on body control and accuracy, until a predetermined goal is reached (e.g., time, number made, positions attempted, etc.).

Coaching Points:

- The kicker's weight should be kept on the balls of his feet. This will hasten his approach speed.

- The kicker should be tested at a variety of angles and forced to adjust his wall-back angle appropriately. The linear concepts of kicking should be reinforced.

- The kicker's plant foot should be checked in relationship to his spot. Often times, a two-step or two-and-half step approach can add discrepancies to the plant foot's location. Plant consistency and location should be worked on.

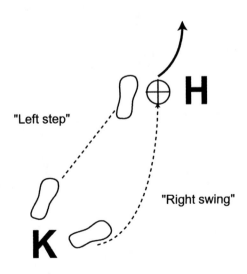

"Left step"

H

"Right swing"

K

Drill #29: COMBINE ELEVATION DRILL

Objective: To test and improve the height of PAT/field-goal kicks; improve level of concentration.

Equipment Needed: A bag of footballs; a goal post.

Description: The holder spots the ball seven yards from the crossbar in the middle of the goal post. The kicker then takes his regular steps and prepares for his kick. The holder simulates the snap when the kicker is ready. The kicker then approaches the ball and executes his kick without trying to compensate for the goal post. The kicker wants to test his elevation from seven yards away. After successfully completing four kicks over the upright, the kicker should move his spot closer by one yard and attempt a series of four kicks at six yards. The drill should be continued until the kicker reaches a point where he cannot successfully elevate the ball. If he continues to elevate the ball well from five yards without overcompensating with his body, he has successfully completed this drill. To add difficulty to the drill, a snapper can be employed in the drill, or the *one-step drill* can be combined with the *elevation drill*.

Coaching Points:

* The kicker should not alter his technique to achieve success in this drill. Only if the kicker has an elevation problem and cannot achieve success from seven yards out, should the kicker work on (and possible adjust) his technique to improve the trajectory of his kicks.

* The kicker should be encouraged to maintain his target line in his follow-through. The straightness of the kick should be tracked. Often times, players who tend to hook their placements can be straightened out by focusing on this drill and its biomechanical requirements for success.

* Maintaining proper eye contact low on the ball is essential to success in this drill.

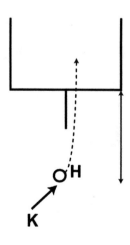

Drill #30: GOAL POST DRILL

Objective: To improve focus and concentration; develop linear principles and improve accuracy; improve elevation.

Equipment Needed: A bag of footballs; a goal post.

Description: The kicker spots his kick 10 yards from the nearest upright along the backline of the end zone. The snapper and holder can be employed to add difficulty and precision to the drill and improve the kicker's level of timing. Beginning kickers may initially wish to do the drill with a grounded placement, or simulated snap. While facing the nearest upright, the kicker then takes his normal steps back, using the upright as his target line. The kicker waits for the snap and executes a kick with the objective of hitting one of the uprights with the kick. His secondary objective is to have the kick land within one yard to the left or right of the backline if the upright is not hit. The drill should be continued for 4-10 kicks, charting each kick for accuracy. A degree of competition can be added to the drill by keeping records of the number of kicks hitting the upright consecutively! This step will add to the challenge of the drill and give the kicker a standard to shoot for each time the drill is run.

Coaching Points:

- The kickers should be encouraged to compete against each other by comparing how many times they can consecutively hit the upright.

- Close attention should be paid to the kicker's body position on his follow-through and its consequences. A close relationship usually exists between the kick's trajectory and a line by the kicker's body position and his follow-through.

- The coach should keep track of the kicker's plant-foot relationship to the ball by noting the proximity of the kicker's plant foot to the back line, where the ball is being spotted.

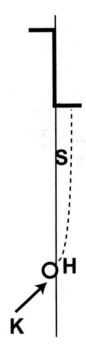

Drill #31: ANGLE KICKING DRILL

Objective: To improve target line; develop proper stepping pattern; improve accuracy on kicks spotted outside the hash marks.

Equipment Needed: A goal post or a target; a bag of footballs.

Description: The kicker and the holder align on the sideline, facing the goal post at the 5-yard line. The kicker will take his steps, trying to remain in perfect alignment with the upright. The drill then begins when the holder spots the ball down, and the kicker executes the kick. The sharpness of the angle he is facing forces the kicker to be precise with his steps and his angle to the ball in order for the ball to be good. Once the kicker has made two consecutive kicks from the 5-yard line, the ball should then be spotted closer to the goal line. If this drill comprises a majority of the kicker's workout, he should slowly progress to the goal line. When this drill is used as a single element of the kicker's workout, he should go directly to the goal post and work to hit two in a row. After doing the drill on one side of the field, the kicker should work the other side.

Coaching Points:

- This is an excellent drill to film, ensuring that the kicker has a chance to see his angle and stepping pattern from the ball. It should be remembered that rear film angles are usually the most helpful.

- The kicker should move closer to the uprights if he is not strong-legged, or is too young to hit from the sideline. The focus of the drill should be on accuracy over power.

- The kicker should be encouraged to develop a small target. This approach will help his steps be more proficient.

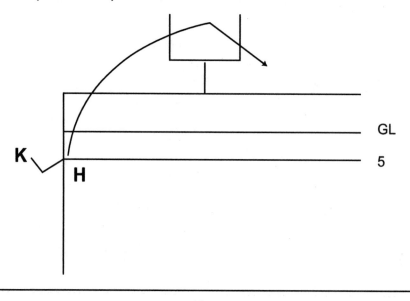

Drill #32: TRASH TALK FIELD GOAL DRILL

Objective: To improve concentration; simulate game-like conditions; develop mental toughness.

Equipment Needed: A bag of footballs.

Description: In this drill, the kicker lines up to execute a kick, while a designated 'harasser' attempts to distract him from his task. The harasser can be vulgar, or matter of fact, in his approach to annoy the kicker. The kicker must block out the disturbance around him and focus solely on making the kick. The harasser should be a team 'character', or someone who knows the kicker well and can get under his skin under normal circumstances. The harasser should stand behind, or beside the kicker, but out of the way of the kick procedure.

Coaching Points:

- Initially, the drill should incorporate a harasser who is at close range. Hopefully, the kicker can begin concentrating at the lower levels of his ability and gradually move back to more challenging kicks.

- The harasser needs to know that he is there to make the kicker better and should strive to find the right buttons to distract the kicker. The kicker should go about his business and "not hear" anything said to him during the drill – regardless of how annoying the harasser becomes.

- Different kinds of harassment should be employed in the drill – from whispering, to false pump-ups (e.g., "you're the best!; you never miss a single kick!; you're all-American!; you won't miss this one!") to add variety to the drill.

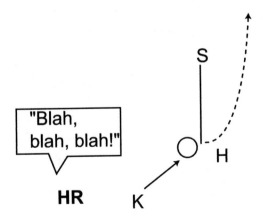

Drill #33: TEAM PRESSURE DRILL

Objective: To improve concentration; simulate game-like conditions; develop mental toughness.

Equipment Needed: Several footballs.

Description: The drill should be done in a team setting without a rush. Team members not involved with the field-goal team stand five yards behind the kicker and make a lot of noise (simulating a crowd). The kicker should do his entire team workout (i.e., six kicks), while under the pressure and distraction of the team behind him. Each kick should be moved to a different location to challenge the kicker in all aspects of his game and to provide variety to the workout.

Coaching Points:

- The kicker should not be told in advance about the team distraction that will take place during practice. The kicker should be encouraged to imagine crowd noise and pressure throughout his workout, especially when he is not in a 'team' setting.

- The coach should watch the kicker's technique as the drill goes on. When kickers lose their level of concentration, the weaknesses in their technique become glaringly obvious. Based on which elements break down, the coach will get a great opportunity to see what needs more drilling and instruction.

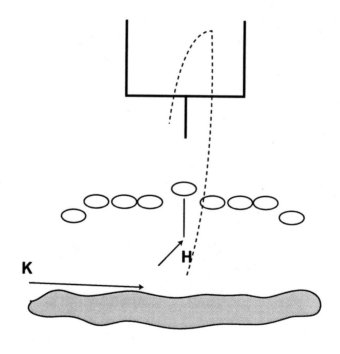

Drill #34: FINDING THE STEPS DRILL

Objective: To improve kickoff stepping pattern, accuracy, and discipline; develop approach consistency.

Equipment Needed: A kickoff tee; a marker (a roll of tape, golf ball, etc.).

Description: It makes no sense for a kicker to mark off his kickoff steps unless he has found his correct starting position. The kicker should first mark a spot where he feels comfortable starting from. The kicker should then go full speed through his steps and execute a kick on air without the use of a tee or a ball. The coach then marks the plant foot's location. The kicker should perform this drill at least five times until a consistent plant foot location is marked. After the correct plant position is found, he should mark off his steps backward until parallel with the starting point (first mark). He should count the steps back until the steps are always the same count. Using a piece of tape, he should then mark the parallel spot and take steps to the side, ending at the origin point. The side steps should be repeated until the step count is always the same. The step off pattern should be repeated several times until it is physically ingrained.

Coaching Points:

- When working on directional kickoffs, make sure that initially the kicker takes angled steps until he knows his exact starting location every time. Once the starting point is found and the kicker is directionally consistent, you can work on disguising his steps.

- The consistency of the kicker taking even steps to map out the walk-off should be stressed.

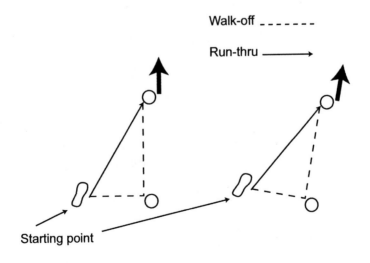

Drill #35: KICKING SCIENTIST DRILL

Objective: To eliminate variables in stepping pattern; improve consistency in approach; develop focus on approach to kickoffs.

Equipment Needed: Several markers (rolls of tape, golf balls, etc.); a kickoff tee.

Description: This drill is intended to help kickers who appear to have different step lengths on their walk-offs. By measuring each step evenly, the coach can eliminate approach and stepping pattern as a problem when analyzing the kicker's technique. After finding the kicker's mark locations from the previous drill (Finding the Steps Drill), smaller markers should be used to measure the step length of the walk-off. This effort should be started by marking each step from the plant foot back. Also, the smaller markers should be employed to mark the kicker's 90-degree (side) steps. After marking each step, the kicker should go through his stepping pattern again, until his steps are within an inch of each marker.

Coaching Points:

- Video taping from the side can be a helpful tool in showing kickers their step deviation.

- Kickers should be encouraged to use the same stride for each step back and each step to the side. The two steps can differ biomechanically, but within each of their elements, they should be the same.

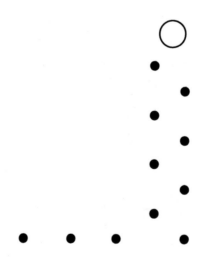

Drill #36: HEADS OR TAILS DRILL

Objective: Improve downward focus and concentration on a kickoff; improve follow-through, stepping pattern, and the technical focus of the kicker; eliminate 'peeking' (premature lifting of the head) in his follow-through.

Equipment Needed: A quarter or half-dollar; a kickoff tee; a bag of footballs.

Description: This simple drill is designed to make the kicker more aware of proper eye focus and the need to concentrate on his follow-through. The drill begins by having the kicker take his regular alignment, straight or directional, and execute his kick as usual. The coach should place down a large coin approximately five yards down the field. When the kicker has executed the kick, he should not lift his eyes to the ball until he has identified what side the coin is on – heads or tails. Upon recognizing the coin, he shouts "heads" or "tails". This drill is excellent as a warm-up drill, or as a dry run-through, without using a ball.

Coaching Points:

- Advanced kickers should describe the kick as they 'feel' it, not as they see it. They can describe how their kick felt and what they think the result of the kick was. This step can help the kicker develop enhanced control through muscle memory.

- Five yards may seem a long distance for most kickers, but if the kicker's follow-through concentration is poor, the exaggerated distance may enhance his ability to eliminate his bad habit.

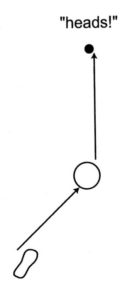

"heads!"

Drill #37: STEPPING LINE DRILL

Objective: To develop or improve the kicker's steps to the ball; enhance concentration and linear visualization skills.

Equipment Needed: Two paper clips with string tied to each end (10 yards of string); a kickoff tee; a bag of footballs.

Description: In this drill, the kicker first measures his steps. When he gets set in his origin point (i.e., where he begins his run up), he should stick one paper clip in the ground, and then stretch the string out and insert the other paper clip in the middle of the plant-foot area (adjacent to the tee). The kicker should practice his run ups and leg swings on air. The string provides a visual stepping reference for the kicker and the coach. When the kicker feels comfortable with his steps and the coach has seen consistency, the string is pulled up and the kicker should kick a set of footballs, while visualizing the string (the line to the ball).

Coaching Points:

- The kicker's body lean should be checked to ensure that his balance is square and even. Often times, an early lean to one side can pull a kicker off the string.

- The steps of the kicker should be tracked. Kickers can gradually improve their approach "alley" by working with the string. This objective can be enhanced if their efforts are videotaped so that they can see where their footwork is deviating from the linear-approach alley.

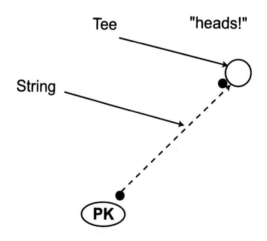

Drill #38: TARGET WARM-UP DRILL

Objective: To warm-up the leg of a kickoff specialist; improve kickoff accuracy; develop linear target concepts.

Equipment Needed: Cones; a bag of footballs; a kickoff tee.

Description: The cones are set up on the 10-yard line (depending on the kicker's strength) on landmarks to the right, left and middle. The kicker tees the ball 10 yards ahead of where he will do so in a game (the 50-yard line for high school kickers). Taking his field-goal steps from his kickoff plant foot area, the kicker then aligns behind the ball and prepares to execute a kick. The kicker should work two kicks to each directional location. After completing one round (six kicks), the kicker then measures his steps from a 5-step approach and executes another round of kicks from five yards back (the 45-yard line for high school kickers). This drill should not be overdone, since overuse injuries are common to kickoff specialists.

Coaching Points:

- The kicker's accuracy should be charted.

- It is essential to emphasize smaller technical aspects, such as opposite arm action, while working the warm-up. Keep in mind, hitting the ball deep is secondary to hitting the targets in this drill.

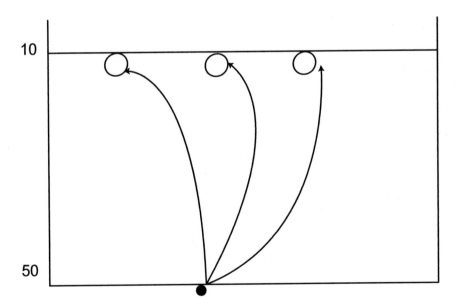

Drill #39: HURDLE VISUALIZATION DRILL

Objective: To develop explosive impact on the ball; enhance follow-through; improve flexibility.

Equipment Needed: A hurdle; a kickoff tee; a bag of footballs.

Description: A hurdle is positioned six yards directly in front of the kickoff tee in line with the desired target. The kicker executes his kickoff and follow-through. As the kicker follows through, he should visualize going over a hurdle. His kicking foot should extend on the follow-through as his leg reaches toward the hurdle. The kicking foot is the first body part to hit the ground after impacting on the ball. The kicker's head should stay focused downward until he sees the hurdle approaching.

Coaching Points:

- The kicker should visualize running over a hurdle with his kicking leg first prior to the kick. This image will give him a muscle memory point to focus on prior to the kick.

- Because this drill is an explosive activity, it is essential that the kicker is loose and stretched prior to exercising.

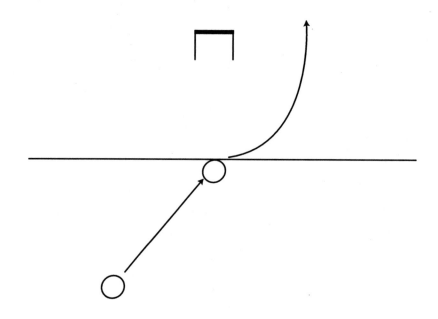

Drill #40: OPPOSITE ARM DRILL

Objective: To fully utilize the opposite arm in the kicking motion; increase awareness of proper kicking technique; improve mechanics; increase power and accuracy.

Equipment Needed: A weighted ball, such as a lacrosse ball or a softball; a kickoff tee; a bag of footballs.

Description: Starting from his final step, the kicker goes through his kicking motion while holding an object in his opposite hand. The kicker wants the ball and his opposite arm to end up in front of his kicking side's shoulder, extended in front of his body. The kicker should kick three or four balls from one step, while focusing on opposite-arm action. Following the one-steps, the kicker should go through his entire kickoff sequence with the ball in his hand. The importance of controlling the opposite arm equally well from one step to the full approach should be emphasized.

Coaching Points:

- The most common problem kickers have in opposite-arm action is maintaining a large arc behind the shoulder plane, which can lead to poor balance and a breakdown in mechanics.

- A relaxed opposite arm is essential. The kicker's grip on the ball should be fairly loose. If the ball is released on the kicker's follow-through, it should be propelled forward at an angle opposite of his arm.

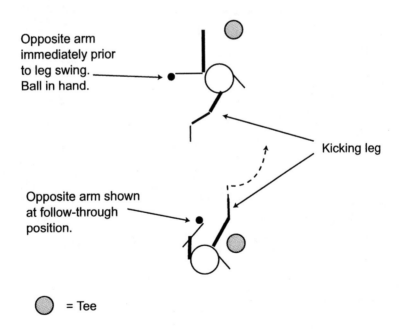

Opposite arm immediately prior to leg swing. Ball in hand.

Kicking leg

Opposite arm shown at follow-through position.

⬤ = Tee

Drill #41: MAY DAY FIELD GOAL DRILL

Objective: To improve a team's ability to get the right personnel on the field to attempt a last second field goal; improve conditioning of the field-goal team; develop and simulate the physical fatigue encountered in a game; develop mental toughness in the kicker.

Equipment Needed: A bag of balls.

Description: In this drill, the coach must have an organized depth chart of his first and second field-goal teams prepared. This step will enable him to make checks and adjustments to any personnel mistakes that could be encountered. It is better to encounter them in this drill than in the game! The drill begins with the first offense running a play from the 30-yard line with 20 seconds remaining and no timeouts. After the play has been executed, a coach (C1) spots the ball in a designated area and yells "may day!" to alert the FIRST field-goal team to rush onto the field. The players not on the field-goal team exit the field. The coach counts down the seconds as they elapse. The FIRST field-goal team must get the snap off before time runs out. After signaling the field goal "good" or "no good", the coach calls "may day" again, and the SECOND field-goal team rushes onto the field. The FIRST field-goal team must then exit the field, and the SECOND field-goal team must execute the 'may day' kick. The cycle continues until each unit has successfully hit five kicks apiece, or until the conditioning aspects of the drill are completed.

Coaching Points:

- ANYONE exiting the field in a 'may day' situation should run BELOW the onrushing field-goal team to enable them to have an unimpeded, straight course to the line of scrimmage.

- Kickers should determine, by the elapsed time, if they have enough time to walk off their kick. If the time is under 10 seconds, the kicker should quickly get himself set in an approximate positioning. He will not have time to get set if he measures his steps.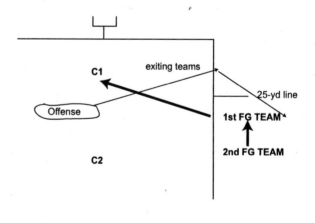

- One coach (C2) should chart the kicks to keep track of each kicker's accuracy under pressure.

CHAPTER 4

DRILLS FOR RETURN SPECIALISTS, HOLDERS AND SNAPPERS

Drill #42: CENTER FIELDER DRILL
(BOTH—KICKOFF RETURNERS AND PUNT RETURNERS)

Objective: To improve jump speed in tracking punts; develop quick reactions; improve catching skills while on the move; prepare specialists for handling good directional punts or kickoffs.

Equipment Needed: A jugs machine, a punter or a quarterback with a strong arm; a football.

Description: In this drill, the return specialist stands in the middle of the field. He needs to be evenly balanced on his toes. His hands should be loose, in front of the stomach. He should be ready to move from side-to-side on a quick jump (somewhat like a basestealer's arms in baseball). The drill begins by having the punter (use a jugs machine if available) step to a directional target and punt the ball. The return man must break quickly to the side and go after the punt, attempting to field the ball cleanly. After catching the ball, the return man should sprint forward, making good juke moves for 10 yards before quickly recovering to the middle of the field. As soon as the return man is back at the starting point, another ball is punted. The punter (jugs) should try to move the return man randomly from side-to-side – keeping him from guessing which way the ball is going. The drill should be repeated as often as needed. This drill can be a specialized conditioning activity as well.

Coaching Points:

- Generally speaking, the more advanced the punter, the easier it will be to determine where the punt is going, because his steps are 'cleaner' – he punts in the direction he steps. Younger punters tend to hit punts that display a more random dispersion. Therefore, it is important to have the return specialist practice both types of kicks.

- The importance of 'reading' the ball off the foot of the punter should be emphasized. This skill is best developed by repping this drill often and getting the return specialist used to seeing the various spins on a football.

Punter/Jugs Machine

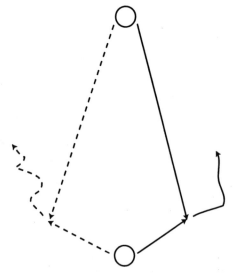

Return specialist

Drill #43: CONCENTRATION AND ALIGNMENT DRILL (BOTH)

Objective: To improve concentration skills; develop manual dexterity; enhance the ability to control body alignment to punted or kicked footballs.

Equipment Needed: A jugs machine or a punter/kicker; footballs.

Description: Holding a football in one hand, the return specialist takes any number of reps using just one hand and body side to catch the football. The return man should focus on seeing the ball with the near eye to the catch side and get his body in perfect alignment to the punt or kick. When fielding a punt, the return specialist should sink slightly at the hips and knees (like a shock absorber). On the kickoff, the specialist should time the catch with a simultaneous roll movement forward on the balls of his feet. The returner should rotate hands and develop each catching side.

Coaching Points:

- With new return men, the drill should begin by tossing the ball with a high trajectory from close range (i.e., 10-15 yards separation). This step will help return specialists to gradually develop confidence in their skills.

- To increase the level of difficulty of this drill, a strip ball component could be added to the drill after the catch is made, or this drill could be combined with the previous drill (Center Fielder Drill).

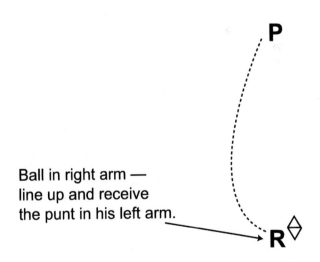

Ball in right arm —
line up and receive
the punt in his left arm.

Drill #44: PUNT/KICK AND TOSS DRILL (BOTH)

Objective: To improve concentration skills; develop manual dexterity; to enhance the ability to control body alignment on punted or kicked footballs.

Equipment Needed: Two or more footballs; a jugs machine or a punter/kicker.

Description: The return specialist aligns downfield and prepares to field a punt or kick. The coach stands 10 yards in front of the return man to one side with a football in hand. The punter/kicker or jugs machine propels the ball downfield to the returner who makes the initial catch. As the ball is being caught, the coach throws his football at an opposite angle toward the return man. The return man must first field the punt and tuck the ball away, and then proceed to catch the coach's throw in his opposite arm. After securing both balls, the return man makes a quick sudden shift and burst move and hands both balls to the coach. The drill is repeated as needed.

Coaching Points:

- It should be reinforced to the return men the importance for carrying the ball in the proper arm, depending on which direction they are running. In this drill, to properly field the second ball, the first ball must be tucked in the correct arm, or it interferes with the return man's ability to get into good position.

- It is important for the return specialist to develop his burst move initially after the second catch, but he should not run with a ball in each arm.

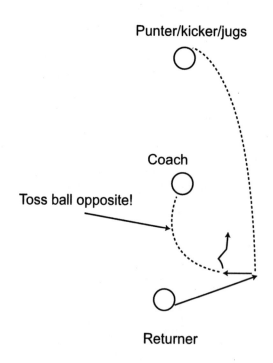

Drill #45: SHADOW DISTRACTION DRILL (BOTH)

Objective: To improve concentration skills; develop manual dexterity; enhance the ability to control body alignment on punted or kicked footballs.

Equipment Needed: A jugs machine or punter/kicker; footballs.

Description: The return specialist aligns at his regular distance to receive a punt or kickoff. The coach or other return men stand 10 yards in front of him. When the ball is propelled, the coach moves into position just one yard in front of the return man and settles down. The coach can tug at the return man's jersey, make noise, or wave his arms in an effort to distract him. The return man must maintain his concentration on the football and not be distracted while catching it. After catching and securing the ball, the return man must make a quick burst move away from the distracter and work upfield.

Coaching Points:

- The distracter must be careful. He should make sure he mimics the movements of the return specialist. If he feels that he may collide with the return man, he should run behind and distract from a safer angle.

- The return man should be required to make a good lateral move upon receiving the catch. The return man can enhance the conditioning aspects of this drill by sprinting various intervals after catching the ball.

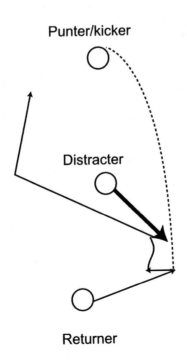

Punter/kicker

Distracter

Returner

Drill #46: ZIG ZAG CUTBACK DRILL (BOTH)

Objective: Develop explosive quickness and change-of-direction skills; improve ball-handling skills.

Equipment Needed: Between six and 12 cones; a football.

Description: In this drill, the ball is kicked or punted to the return man. Upon receiving the ball, the return man accelerates forward 10 yards and breaks to the first cone. When reaching the first cone, he makes a quick lateral change of direction, chopping his feet in his cut while preparing to switch the ball to his other arm. The drill continues until the return man has negotiated the course. After the final cone, he sprints straight ahead for a minimum of 10 yards (the coach can have him go all the way if the coach wants).

Coaching Points:

- Some coaches do not like return men switching the ball while they run – that decision is up to each individual program's philosophy.

- The cone alignments can be mixed and matched. Changing them up after each run will provide variety and challenge to your specialists. It also is more realistic to the game's varieties.

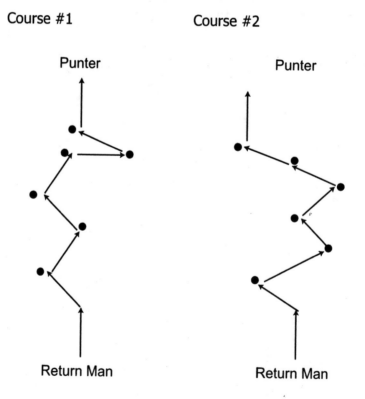

Course #1   Course #2

Punter   Punter

Return Man   Return Man

Drill #47: ESCAPE FROM ALCATRAZ DRILL (BOTH)

Objective: To improve dexterity in a confined space; develop balance; increase foot quickness; provide a realistic, game-like situation in a controlled environment.

Equipment Needed: Six cones; a football.

Description: Cones are set up in a rectangle, evenly spaced five yards apart. The return men stand on one end of the rectangle while the coverage men stand on the opposite side. The coach stands behind the coverage men. The drill begins with the coach simulating a kick or punt with a toss to the first return man. Upon receiving the ball, the first coverage man attacks the return man. The goal is for the return man to beat the coverage man with effective juke, stiff arm, or speed moves and finish the drill by running through the far cones. If he 'scores', the return line gets a point. If he is tackled or forced outside the cones, the coverage line gets a point. A predetermined number of points "wins" the competition.

Coaching Points:

- The drill can be made easier or harder for the respective players by manipulating the width or length of the cone alignments.

- The level of contact (i.e., thud, live) is dependant upon a team's practice philosophy.

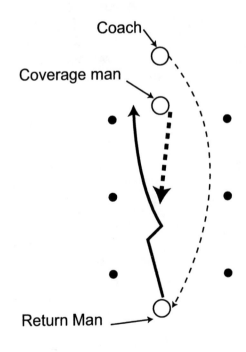

Drill #48: ROLLING INTO THE KICKOFF DRILL (KICK RETURNERS)

Objective: Teach return men to properly field a kickoff; develop dexterity; increase concentration skills under pressure; increase explosive separation and acceleration skills.

Equipment Needed: A jugs machine or kicker; a bag of footballs.

Description: In this drill, a line of return specialists receiving kickoffs is positioned on a starting line. The drill is begun by having the coach stand 20 yards from the starting line and tossing a ball, end-over-end, that consistently falls five yards in front of the starting line. The return men roll forward on their toes and get their bodies working toward the thrown ball. The return men want to time their speed with the catch at the five-yard mark. Upon receiving the ball, the returner sprints 10 yards forward, and then breaks to the right or left as specified by the coach. After each returner has caught two balls, a kicker or jugs machine should be used to better simulate game conditions. The kicker should work on 'spot' kicks to specific distances and locations.

Coaching Points:

- The return men should work their hands and eyes in this drill. They should receive the ball with their hands, carefully bringing the ball into a good secure position as they move forward.

- New return men should gradually increase the distance of their run-ups. They should work to catch the ball just below their eyes. This technique will help ensure that they will use the ideal reception point (their middle chests) to catch the ball since the ball will drop as the players are working toward it. Keep in mind that as a rule, it is easier to catch a high ball than a low ball.

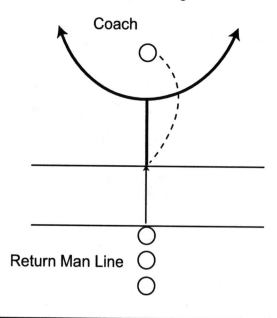

Drill #49: DECISION DRILL (PUNT RETURNERS)

Objective: To improve field awareness; develop good decision-making skills when fielding punts in the critical area (+50 punts).

Equipment Needed: A punter or jugs machine; a bag of footballs.

Description: In this drill, the return man aligns on the 8-yard line and prepares to field a pooch, or "+50" punt. He should prepare to make this catch by getting in a good returner's stance – his weight balanced on the toes, his knees bent and his hands in proper position (like a basestealer's). When the punt is made, the returner begins describing his movement ("back" for any backward movement, "up" for any forward movement), while concentrating on receiving the punt. He must continuously recite his direction as he awaits the punt. If the return man says, "back" more than twice, he should move away from the punt and signal a fair catch as a decoy. If he makes no calls, he must decide what call to make based on the height of the punt. On punts where he calls "up" more than three times, he should signal fair catch as the safe option. Other options can be added to the drill, based on a program's philosophy.

Coaching Points:

- The most important aspect of this drill is that all punts should be handled cleanly. The return man should adjust his calls, such as "Peter" or "Paul", based on what his team uses.

- Younger players should practice making calls without the ball, based on their movement. This 'reverse' return drill can help punt returners establish good habits under pressure.

Punter/jugs machine

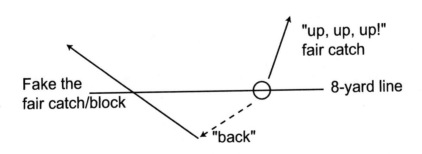

Drill #50: SPEED ROTATION DRILL

Objective: To improve a holder's ability to properly spin the ball; develop good hand-eye coordination; increase the level of feel for the ball.

Equipment Needed: A football.

Description: The holder gets into his ideal position and aligns his tee or his spot on the ground. The coach kneels an arm's length in front of the holder. The holder goes through a mock check off with the kicker, then looks to the center, and calls for the ball. Hiding the football behind his back with one hand, the coach brings the ball up to the holder's hand. The holder takes the ball from the coach and spots the ball, rotating the laces when necessary. Immediately after placement of the ball, the holder hands the ball back to the coach. The coach can realign the laces to challenge the holder and adjust the pace of the drill as needed.

Coaching Point:

• The coach can either have the holder recheck with the kicker prior to each handoff, or go rapid fire, continuously handing the ball back to the holder once his spot is reset and he calls for the ball.

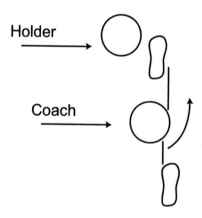

Holder

Coach

Drill #51: ALIGNMENT DRILL

Objective: To develop good field sense and alignment to the upright; improve understanding of the importance of the kicking line to the holder; improve lace orientation.

Equipment Needed: A tee (if used).

Description: The kicker (or coach) will move around the field, placing his spots. The holder must jog to the location of the spot (preferably from the sideline), kneel, and align his body properly to the upright. The kicker or coach then provides feedback to the holder to help him get into a perfect relationship to the uprights and with the target line. After the drill has been run several times, the holder should develop a pattern for self-alignment, using his own body position and hands to check himself.

Coaching Points:

- Once the holder gets set with his knees and feet, he should take his near hand to the center (i.e., the right hand for a right-footed kicker) and trace the line from his back knee to his front foot. The knee and foot should be aligned directly down the center of the uprights (parallel to the kicker's target line).

- The importance of proper alignment by the holder to the linear philosophy of the kicking motion should be emphasized. Everyone must be aligned straight to lessen the margin of error.

Drill #52: BAD SNAP RECOVERY DRILL

Objective: To improve hands and timing on poor snaps; develop good decision-making skills; enhance calmness and hands under pressure.

Equipment Needed: A bag of footballs.

Description: In this drill, the holder and coach properly align, and the snapper gives the coach the ready signal. The coach goes over the proper calls on bad snaps (i.e., a "fire" call) and tells the holder the game situation. This technique helps to reinforce the holder's thought process on game day. The holder calls for the ball, and the coach snaps the ball erratically. The holder must try to get the ball successfully spotted for kick, but if he cannot do so, he is to execute the team's emergency call. This drill continues for 5-10 minutes.

Coaching Points:

- Good snaps should be mixed with the bad to maintain the holder's focus on getting the ball down first.

- Over time, the holder's weak areas should be worked the hardest in this drill. For instance, most holders have a more difficult time with balls snapped low and to their backsides. In this instance, an effort should be made to develop the holder's weaknesses, in addition to working on his emergency calls.

Scenario #1: Emergency call – no hold   Scenario #2: Successful hold

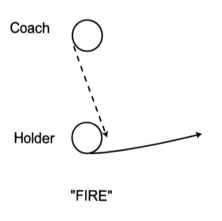

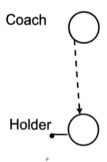

Drill #53: PENNY ACCURACY DRILL

Objective: To improve spot consistency; develop hand-eye coordination; apply added pressure to holding in practice; increase the holder's level of feel for the ball.

Equipment Needed: A football; a penny.

Description: In this drill, the holder takes a coin out to spot the ball. If the spot is made on a tee, the coin is placed in the middle of the tee. After the holder has spotted his coin down and is in proper alignment, he calls for the ball. He must try to put the ball down directly on top of the coin each time. Every ball that does not land on the coin will be recorded by how far it is away from the coin. If the direction of the miss – front, back, left, or right – is included in the record-keeping efforts, a definite pattern of the holder will develop. This pattern can then be used to help the holder adjust his hands to the perfect angle when he spots each kick. For instance, if he averages two inches to the right of his spot, he should adjust his body position to where his average hold comes down – two inches over.

Coaching Point:

- If the holder spots the ball all over the place, this drill should be done on a regular basis every practice. On the other hand, if the holder is consistently missing by a small margin, he should work on making the adjustment without moving his relationship to the spot.

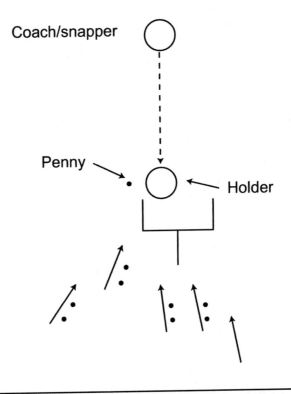

Drill #54: QUICK SNAPS DRILL

Objective: To develop good hand-eye coordination; increase the level of feel for the ball; improve consistency under pressure; improve hand speed around the ball.

Equipment Needed: A bag of footballs; a snapper or coach to snap or underhand launch the balls.

Description: In this drill, the holder gets his mark, and a snapper or coach aligns at regular snapping distance and alignment. To start the drill, the holder first checks with a 'pretend' kicker before calling for the ball. The first ball is then snapped, and the holder must spot the ball and rotate the laces as quickly as possible. After the ball has been held for a full count, the holder pushes the ball off to the side and calls for another snap. He continues this process until all the balls in the bag have been used.

Coaching Points:

- The holder must get the ball placed properly and must hold the ball past the kicker's get-off time (don't allow the holder to develop a bad habit for the sake of speed).

- The importance of calling for the ball and focusing on each individual ball in the drill being held perfectly should be emphasized.

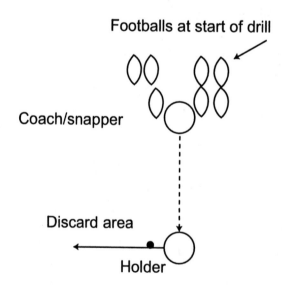

Footballs at start of drill

Coach/snapper

Discard area

Holder

Drill #55: HEAVY BALL WARM-UP DRILL

Objective: To warm-up the snapper; improve the snapper's grip; strengthen and condition the muscles specific to deep snapping.

Equipment Needed: A Wilson heavy football or a ball wrapped with metal tape.

Description: In this drill, the heavy ball is held over the head of the snapper in the position covered in the next drill (Two Thumbs Up – Two Thumbs Down). The snapper works to spiral the ball to a specific target on a partner, while thrusting himself up on his toes. His thumbs should finish down to the ground when he is standing and up at the sky from underneath. When snapping from his normal position, it is important that the holder stand a maximum of seven yards away and provides a target (i.e., his Adam's apple) for the deep snapper to aim. This drill is another exercise that can be done for punt, or short snappers. The snapper should perform 5-10 perfect snaps from each position. This step will develop his overall stamina and increase the power in his snap.

Coaching Points:

- It is essential that the punter should stand seven yards behind the snapper for punt snaps is key because the heavy ball will naturally sink at 12-13 yards. With the punter standing at seven yards and offering his Adam's apple as a target, the snapper is more likely to develop good aiming and trajectory habits, while developing explosive power.

- Incorporating the holder into the short-snap drill will help him to develop softer, sturdier hands. Keep in mind that a punter or kicker should <u>never</u> kick the heavy ball.

Drill #56: TWO THUMBS DOWN – TWO THUMBS UP DRILL

Objective: To develop good follow-through habits in a long snapper; improve the focus and concentration on proper technique; condition the muscles used in a deep-snap operation.

Equipment Needed: None.

Description: In this drill, the snapper is working to increase the speed and form of his snap operation. From the standing position, the snapper holds his hands over his head. His hands should be cocked as if he is snapping a ball, at the proper alignment. His non-throwing hand should be on the bottom seam of the ball, with the top of the hand directly over his head. His throwing hand should be positioned on the ideal throwing spot of the individual snapper. The snapper should then rapid fire his hands at a target and rotate his thumbs downward, finishing with "two thumbs down" on each follow-through. This drill should be repeated 10 times in the rapid-fire mode. He should then rest for 10 seconds and repeat the exercise. After repeating this drill as needed, the drill should be performed from a football stance. Each individual follow-through should be executed as it would be done in a game situation, losing ground slightly with the force of the follow-through, while rapid firing the hands between the legs. "Two thumbs up" is the object from this angle.

Coaching Points:

- Some coaches use ankle, or wrist weights (one pound or less) to develop strength in the snapping motion. Aerobics weights are ideal.

- If the snapper is unsure how to position his hands in the drill, he should be given a ball to position over his head, or underneath him. The ball should then be removed immediately prior to beginning the drill.

Drill #57: QUICK SNAP DRILL

Objective: To warm-up the snapper; improve snaps under pressure; improve snaps in a time-sensitive situation; develop quick target sighting and reaction skills.

Equipment Needed: Three or more footballs.

Description: Three balls are aligned in a straight line, approximately three-yards apart. The snapper begins on the sideline and runs on the field with a "go" call from the coach. The snap can be either long or short for this drill. When the snapper runs onto the field, he quickly gets over the first ball and snaps it to either the coach or the player behind him. After snapping the first ball, he moves over the next ball in the line and snaps it after locating his target. He proceeds to the third ball and finishes the drill with another snap. After finishing the drill, the snapper and coach go over the snap areas and work to develop more consistency with each snap.

Coaching Points:

- After executing the drill once or twice from a straight line, the footballs can be organized in various patterns in order to have the snapper face even more demanding challenges as he moves to the next football in line.

- This drill can be used to develop game-like fatigue in the snapper. Generally speaking, on the last snap of this drill, most snappers will be fatigued as they will be late in a game. It is crucial that the snapper focus and concentrate as he becomes fatigued.

Drill with balls in a line   Drill with footballs staggered

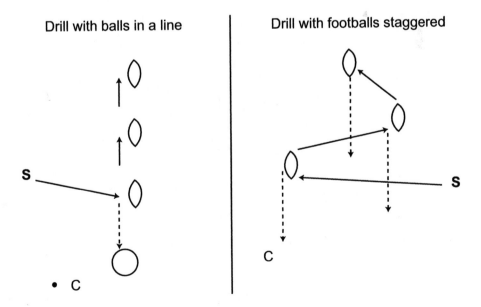

Drill #58: UPRIGHT TARGET PRACTICE DRILL

Objective: To improve accuracy and consistency; develop good aiming habits; apply proper techniques in a pressure situation in practice.

Equipment Needed: A bag of footballs; an upright or a fence with aiming marks taped or drawn.

Description: This drill is a simple exercise designed to improve the targeting capabilities of a deep snapper. Using an object, such as an upright or a fence, a snapper marks various locations, including a punter's belt (three feet), and the snapper's hand (one foot high). After marking out his snap locations, the snapper should snap balls into the object until he has consistently hit the target. The snapper should do a pre-determined number of snaps during this drill each day and strive for 100% accuracy. A chart may be kept displaying snap accuracy.

Coaching Points:

- If the coach prefers to have a snapper who snaps blind, this is an excellent target acquisition drill.

- This drill is a great exercise for snappers to work on during the off-season, or if they need to work on something on their own.

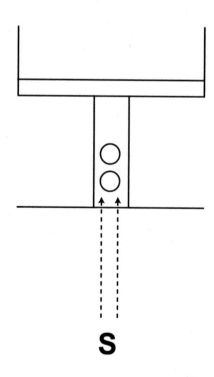

Drill #59: FLAT BACK DRILL

Objective: To demonstrate and improve body positioning of the long snapper; increase concentration; improve technique.

Equipment Needed: A 10-pound universal weight; a bag of footballs.

Description: In this drill, the coach places a 5- or 10- pound plate from a weight room on the lower back of a snapper who is over the ball in a good snapping position. The snapper goes through his snaps in a warm-up situation with the weight on his back. The snapper should then perform 5-10 snaps consecutively, while attempting to keep the weight from either falling off to either side or sliding down his backside.

Coaching Points:

- If the weight falls off to the right, the snapper is too right-hand dominant and is only using his right side to snap the ball. Snaps will be pulled right if not corrected.

- If the plate falls off to the left, the snapper is either leaning too far to the left, or is too left-hand dominant and needs to balance himself in his follow-through. In this situation, snaps will go left.

- If the plate falls off behind, the snapper either is too high on his follow-through or is raising his head up early (easier for a rush to defeat). He needs to keep his back flat at all times. This scenario can also indicate a snapper who is snapping too low.

- If the weight rolls toward the snapper's shoulder pad, the snapper's butt is too high, which can lead to high snaps!

10-pound plate

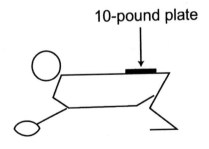

Drill #60: SNAP AND SLIDE PROTECTION DRILL

Objective: To develop proper footwork in punt snappers; increase foot quickness; teach good technique.

Equipment Needed: A football; marked turf (cones or tape).

Description: Areas of the ground are marked with tape or cones. The marking begins with the snapping point. Next, the ground is marked two yards behind and two yards over (right or left). Mark another area two yards behind the second mark and four yards over (opposite the direction of the first mark). The course is completed by marking a spot five yards directly behind the origin point. The drill is initiated by having the snapper execute a punt snap. After snapping the ball, the snapper should kick slide to the first marker, then redirect to the second marker, and finish by sliding to the final point directly behind where he began. After executing this drill several times, the drill should be performed several more times in reverse order of the sliding marks until the footwork patterns are well run.

Coaching Points:

- The snapper should be required to remain low and maintain a wide base (shoulder-width apart). The ideal body position and hand position for the snapper may vary according to a program's standards.

- To condition snappers, the snapper should engage in his drop-step pattern for any predetermined number of yards. The coach can be creative and design courses that encourage good change-of-direction skills in his snapper.

- In evaluating snappers and their ability to make blocks, the coach can design and use a course and time each snapper's ability to complete the course. This technique will give the coach a footwork pecking order from which to choose.

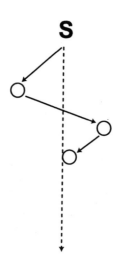

PART III

TEAM
DRILLS

CHAPTER 5

PUNT DRILLS

Drill #61: HAND CHECK/AWARENESS DRILL

Objective: To improve blocking skills; develop 'team' awareness within each player on the punt team; enhance techniques on the line of scrimmage; teach players to play on either side of the punt team.

Equipment Needed: A football.

Description: In this drill, each player begins from the guard position on the punt team. The punt team player has two rush players in front of him — one inside gap player and one outside technique (anywhere from head-up to positioned over a ghost tackle). On the snap of the ball, the punt team player fires his inside hand into the inside rusher and executes his steps to recover to the outside player (or his assignment in the protection scheme). The drill is completed when the outside man is correctly blocked. The inside player rushes until he is hand-checked by the guard. If the guard does not properly hand-check the inside rusher, he continues to the block point (showing the coach that he was not checked initially and forcing the guard to attempt a 1-on-2 block). The drill should be repeated for players on both sides, but everyone should be cycled through BOTH sides of the drill.

Coaching Points:

- Coaches can modify this drill for tackles and wings also. For example, inactive players can be used on the line to allow for proper splits and to serve as 'stand-ins' as the play runs.

- In the beginning, the drill should focus on the initial step/shuffle and hand check. This approach will reinforce the drill's emphasis to the players, while enhancing their technique early in punt protection.

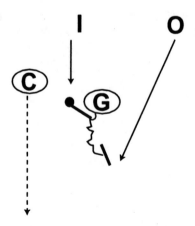

Drill #62: LINE STEPPING DRILL

Objective: To improve blocking skills; develop 'team' awareness within each player on the punt team; enhance body positioning on the line of scrimmage; teach players to play on either side of the punt team.

Equipment Needed: A lined field.

Description: The punt team players assemble on three selected yard lines that are five yards apart (e.g., 15, 20, 25) facing the coach. There can be as many as four on each line, provided that the players are spaced at least two yards from the back of the player in front of them. The drill begins by having the coach inform the players where the ball is (to the right or left). The players put their outside feet on the line, and assume their stance and hold until the coach's "go" command. On the coach's command or whistle, the players execute their stepping pattern (e.g., kick-slide), while staying under control and in correct posture. Ideally, a kick-slide blocker will begin with his outside foot on the yard line and end with his inside foot on the line. The coach should repeat the drill and walk among the players to see that all are executing their steps properly. After each player has mastered their correct steps, the location of the center/ball should be switched. Players should learn proper stepping patterns of both sides.

Coaching Points:

- Depending on the scheme, collapsing or fanning protection, the coach may wish to switch which foot of the players he wants on the line to begin and end the drill.

- The drill can be manipulated depending on how many steps a team is taking and the location the coach wants the players to be at the completion of the drill. The main advantage of this drill is that the coach can check individual footwork relatively quickly while the players are performing several reps.

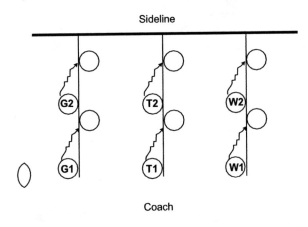

G — Guard, T—Tackle, W—Wing/slot (kickside drill shown)

Drill #63: TEAM STEP DRILL

Objective: To improve blocking skills; develop 'team' awareness within each player on the punt team; enhance body positioning on the line of scrimmage; teach players to play on either side of the punt team.

Equipment Needed: A football.

Description: The players align in two punt groups. The first group assumes a position on the line of scrimmage and gets into their proper alignments. The calls are made, and the ball is snapped to the punter. On the snap of the ball, the punt team executes their steps and hand-checks and freezes on their last steps. On the freeze, the coaches have time to check the alignment of the punt team at impact point (when the ball hits the punter's foot). After the first group has been critiqued, they go to the back of the line, and the second unit takes a snap. The drill continues until the coaches have seen the results they are looking for from the players. For variety, rapid fire this drill and stop the exercise after each group has executed their steps perfectly a predetermined number of times.

Coaching Points:

- Teams that emphasize their protection first will benefit from this drill and its emphasis on each player's location in the protection scheme. This drill also helps players get a good feel for their location.

- This drill can be modified for a particular protection scheme. Every scheme has a point of balance, where the players shift from protection to coverage (usually as a unit). In these schemes, the transfer point should be the 'freeze' point in this drill.

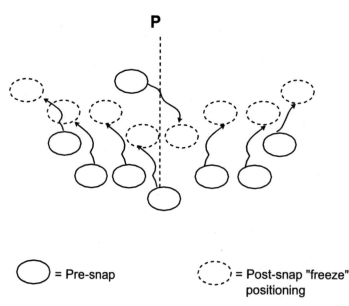

= Pre-snap   = Post-snap "freeze" positioning

Drill #64: HALF-LINE STUNT/TWIST/STACK DRILL

Objective: To teach zone and man blocking principles and assignments; develop good footwork and concentration; provide the coach with an accurate assessment of protection personnel.

Equipment Needed: A football.

Description: This drill uses half of a line, from center to tackle, and a fullback/ personal protector. If a team has enough staff, another coach can be incorporated into the drill to take the opposite side of the line, along with the second snapper and fullback/personal protector. This drill also requires a rush team, which can be comprised of either the first punt team's back-up players or the scout team members. The drill begins with the punt team getting into alignment and getting set. The coach stands behind the punt team and signals the scout team's look. The coach can align the scout team anywhere he wants and run any combination of stacks, twists, or overloads. When the scout team has their assignment, they get into their stance, and the fullback makes the correct calls and adjustments. The ball is snapped, and the half-line executes their protection against the called scout-team play. After executing their block, the punt team works to get free of their assignment and begins their course downfield, stopping at the line of scrimmage. After the rep, they get back on the line quickly, listen to coach's analysis, and get into their stance for another rep.

Coaching Points:

- Cards can be used for the scout team to create a faster pace for this drill. This drill is a great exercise to rep an opponent's favorite stunt look or work at a walk-through pace prior to the punt team practice.

- If a team employs a man/zone scheme, basic 3-man or 4-man looks can be worked on to rehearse each player's assignment prior to running the more complex stunts.

- The center and fullback may not have an assignment, depending upon the call. They should work hard on their steps and help other players if they are free, especially the fullback.

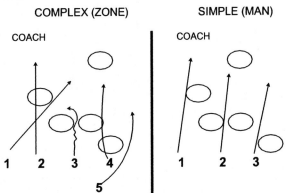

COMPLEX (ZONE)   SIMPLE (MAN)

Drill #65: STEPS-N-HIT IT DRILL

Objective: To improve footwork; develop 'team' awareness within each player on the punt team; enhance body positioning on the line of scrimmage; improve coverage awareness.

Equipment Needed: A football. (Dots optional).

Description: This drill utilizes the entire punt team as a whole and is run on air. The emphasis is in getting the entire unit to step together in their protection and work to coverage with the understanding of their role in space (the open field) and initial downfield coverage. The drill begins with the first punt team hurrying onto the field and getting set. Following the calls, the ball is snapped, and the players take their steps as if they were blocking a 'zone' side. After stepping, the players hit the ground in a push-up position and then spring back up, quickly emerging to their coverage areas (some coaches call them "lanes", while others refer to them as "responsibilities"). The drill is completed when the team has covered to 10 yards. After the first group has finished, the second punt group gets on the ball quickly and executes the drill. The drill continues until the coach is satisfied with the steps and coverage of each group. If players find difficulty in getting to the proper coverage area at the drill's completion, dots could be placed that correspond with each player at the drill's ending point (10 yards).

Coaching Points:

- The drill can be modified to include full coverage or force players to avoid various downfield blocks/obstacles. If pads cannot be utilized in a particular practice, this drill most closely simulates a punt with game-like situations (i.e., potentially hitting the ground).

- The coach should focus on the player's fan or coverage response to the various punts kicked. He should make his coverage adjustments on the field by repositioning players at the completion of the drill.

Drill #66: DOTS COVERAGE DRILL

Objective: To improve coverage responsibilities; develop continuity in coverage; enable players to use their hands to eliminate blockers.

Equipment Needed: A few footballs; a punter or a jugs machine.

Description: Eight dots are positioned equidistance apart 10 yards downfield from the punt line of scrimmage. The gunners align at their regular locations and have double press (i.e., two defenders in front), making it difficult for them to get out into coverage. The players are positioned on a dot according to their coverage responsibility at the 10-yard mark. Their back-ups should stand behind them (next in line), and a scout group to hold-up and disrupt the coverage men should stand immediately in front of each coverage player. The return men stand at a regular depth to receive and return each punt. A person to snap the ball to the punter who is not involved in punt coverage can be used to start the drill (either a third snapper or the coach). The drill leader (coach) stands 10 yards in front of the coverage players and blow a whistle to start the drill by having the ball snapped to the punter. The punter (jugs) punts the ball, and, as the ball goes over the head of the drill leader, signals and points to the right, left, or both sides of coverage players to cover the punt. On the command, the coverage players must get off the blocks of the hold-up people and cover to the ball. The drill is completed when the return man is corralled, or tagged off. The return men should work on their change of direction and speed moves, making it difficult for the coverage to make the play.

Coaching Points:

* To give the coverage the right idea, it may be desirable to run this drill without any hold-up players at first and subsequently add them to increase the difficulty.

* The gunners may release on the snap of the ball. They should work their 2-on-1 moves to get off the line of scrimmage.

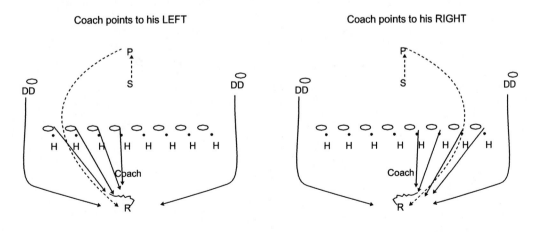

Coach points to his LEFT   Coach points to his RIGHT

Drill #67: ESCAPE FROM ALCATRAZ GUNNER DRILL

Objective: To improve and develop wide receiver/gunner footwork in punt coverage; develop decision-making skills; recreate game conditions and speed in a rapid repetition drill.

Equipment Needed: Two cones.

Description: The gunner is aligned on the line of scrimmage and two cones are positioned 2.5 yards apart on either side of him. Two corner backs, or defenders are aligned on the other side of the line of scrimmage. Coach stands to the inside of the gunner and moves a ball to simulate a snap. On the snap, the gunner attempts to release from the line, and the defenders have the mission of pinning him down – using their body position and hands to hold-up the gunner. The drill is completed when either the gunner gets past the defenders successfully, or the gunner is stopped by the defenders.

Coaching Points:

- The proper use of hands in avoiding and getting freedom from blocks downfield should be emphasized. The secondary emphasis should be on speed burst at the line of scrimmage and in downfield avoidance.

- Score can be kept to determine the best defenders and gunners.

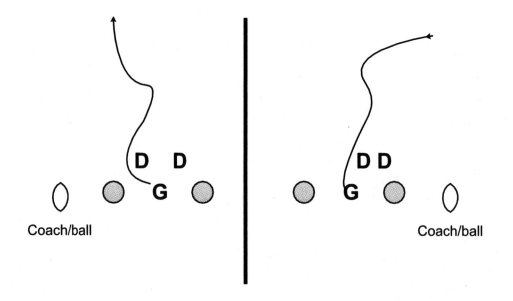

Drill #68: STACKED DECK GUNNER DRILL

Objective: To improve and develop wide receiver/gunner footwork in punt coverage; develop decision-making skills; recreate game conditions and speed in a rapid repetition drill.

Equipment Needed: Three cones.

Description: The gunner is aligned on the line of scrimmage and two cones are positioned 2.5 yards apart on either side of him. Two corner backs, or defenders, are aligned on the other side of the line of scrimmage, and a third player assumes a position 10 yards down the field. The coach stands to the inside of the gunner and moves a ball to simulate a snap. On the snap, the gunner attempts to release from the line and the defenders have the mission of pinning him down – using their body position and hands to hold-up the gunner. When the gunner gets five yards downfield, the two defenders have finished their part of the drill. The gunner then progresses to the second-level player (i.e., the third defender), who works to position himself to block the gunner from a side angle downfield. The drill is completed when either the gunner gets past the third defender successfully, or the gunner is stopped by any of the defenders.

Coaching Points:

- Sometimes it can be fun to create a one-on-one initially and place two defenders in various points down the field to provide variety to the drill and make it a more game-like environment.

- Score can be kept with the gunners and defenders. In this instance, the coach may find that some players dominate at each position.

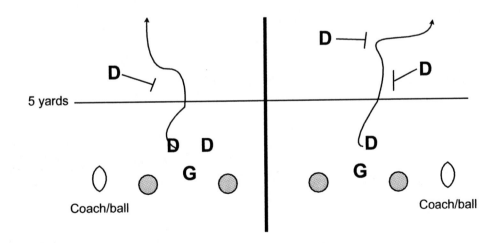

89

Drill #69: POOCH DRILL - GUNNERS

Objective: To teach gunners how to play punts in the +50 (pooch) zone; develop good receiving habits; improve decision-making skills; develop the punter's feel for directional/pooch punting.

Equipment Needed: A bag of footballs.

Description: This drill involves two punters — one standing on the right hash mark and the other on the left on the 50-yard line. Half of the footballs are given to each punter. Two lines of gunners, on either side of the punters, align on the college numbers on the 35-yard line. The punters simultaneously spin the ball in their hands and call "go", signaling the gunners (i.e., the wide receivers) to release downfield. The punters kick the ball, looking to drop the ball on the eight-yard line near the college numbers. At the 20-yard line, the gunner locates the punted football and makes a decision to: 1) catch the ball, 2) bat the ball out of the end zone, or 3) let the ball roll while protecting his end zone. If the ball accidentally touches the gunner, he must recover the ball as quickly as possible (first-touch rule). Each gunner should go twice on each side. After executing this drill on air, a hold-up player on each gunner can be added, as well as a return specialist to work on his calls/decisions. The drill can be moved back five yards and the spot of the ball varied to simulate game-like surroundings.

Coaching Points:

- The coach should be patient in the progression of the drill from performing it "on air" to adding corners, return men, and other players to this drill. He should ensure that his gunners are repeatedly seeing many kinds of pooch punts and making the right decisions/catches.

- This drill can be a good directional warm-up drill in pre-practice for punters. Punters do not need to kill the ball; they simply need to work on good, consistent directional punts.

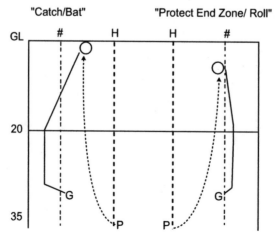

Drill #70: FULLBACK/PROTECTOR DECISION DRILL

Objective: To combat interior stunting by punt-rush teams; develop good decision-making skills; teach good blocking techniques and habits; improve punt-team communication; provide a pressure-filled drill for fullbacks/protectors.

Equipment Needed: A deep snapper; a bag of footballs.

Description: In this drill, four players are aligned either on or within one gap of the deep snapper, balanced, or overloaded as directed by the coach. The coach stands behind the fullback and gives each of the four players an option, not limited to the following: 1) drop off the line of scrimmage, 2) rush straight, 3) rush angle, 4) stunt/loop around, or 5) grab either the DS, or the FB. The fullback determines which direction he wants to block (or send the center). The fullback makes the appropriate directional call to the center, who then snaps the ball. The center and fullback must work in tandem to protect and release into coverage. The drill is completed when either the DS or the FB breaks down in their assignments, or they complete the drill successfully by releasing 10 yards.

Coaching Points:

- In some protection schemes, the center does not block. In those cases, the snapper should just send the ball back and release. The coach can have two of the four "rush-look" players resist the center at the LOS.

- At first, only two players should rush. This technique will give the DS and FB the right concept of protection. After they have mastered this factor, the FB should be forced to pick-up two rushers (i.e., a disaster scenario), and the team required to work against various twists and stunts that they often face.

- For college or pro coaches, this drill is ideal for practicing cut blocks. If cutting is an option, it is recommended that a segment of this drill be done using light, full-size dummies, or shields that can be done by the look team to give a target/ protect themselves in the drill.

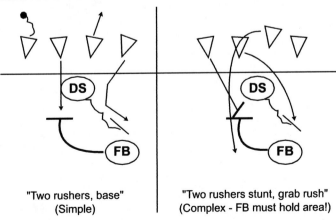

"Two rushers, base"   "Two rushers stunt, grab rush"
(Simple)   (Complex - FB must hold area!)

CHAPTER 6

PUNT RETURN DRILLS

Drill #71: PUNT BLOCK ON A MAT DRILL

Objective: To develop exceptional hand-eye coordination; improve timing in blocking a punt; develop an understanding of block point; reduce the likelihood of penalties, such as roughing or running into the punter.

Equipment Needed: A gym mat (6-foot square); a football or volleyball.

Description: In reality, some coaches teach never leaving your feet in a punt block situation. On the other hand, one of the primary reasons players rough the punter or miss a block opportunity is due to a lack of hand-eye coordination and a poor understanding of block point. Both of these factors can be improved through practice. In this drill, laying out in front of the block point is used as an acceptable means of blocking a punt. First, a piece of tape is used to mark an 'X' on the ground where the block point exists. Next, the outside punt block specialists (the 'speed' guys) form a line five yards from the 'X'. A mat is placed on the ground two feet away from the block point 'X', in a direct line with the player's line. A punter or the coach stands three yards from block point ready to "punt" the ball. On the movement of the punter, the players run half-speed to the "X", while eyeing the ball (actually looking at the side of the ball closest to them). The player extends his arms, keeping his hands together, and lays out over top of the "X", while keeping his eyes focused on the ball. The player then lands on the mat and deflects the ball. After hitting the mat, the player springs up on his feet, locates the ball, and runs to it.

Coaching Points:

- Using a volleyball teaches players to look to the center of the ball, not the front point. This is an important aiming location in blocking kicks.

- Depending on the speed of the players, they may need to stand back 10 yards to receive adequate timing in this drill. While laying out may not always be the most ideal way to block a punt, with an emphasis placed on WHERE to lay out each week, players will greatly improve their ability to avoid contact with the punter.

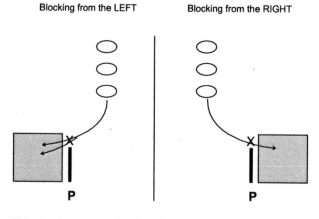

Blocking from the LEFT   Blocking from the RIGHT

** Angles shown using a right-footed punter.

Drill #72: 1-V-1 PUNT BLOCK DRILL

Objective: To develop punt rush moves; improve economy of footwork; encourage the use of a block point in rushing punts.

Equipment Needed: A football.

Description: The drill employs a scout team punt unit that assembles in the formation of a team's weekly opponent. The punter's block point is labeled using colored tape or a dot. Most block points are between nine and 11 yards behind the line of scrimmage. The coach selects the player he wants to begin the drill with. That player ('A') gets into an aggressive stance and peers in on the ball. The ball is then moved by the snapper. Player 'A' explodes over his man, working either a speed burst, rip, swim, or quick move. After achieving quick separation from the scout team player, player 'A' works to get to the block point. All players should run through the block point with their hands in good positioning. After 'A' runs through the block point, the coach can designate another rusher. The drill cycles until all players have run through the block point, while executing a good punt-rush move.

Coaching Points:

- Most coaches begin the drill by working on a specific pass-rush move. After one cycle is completed, the move is then changed to provide players with a 'package' of moves from which to choose.

- Adding a punter or working rushers against a 2-v-1 (zone block) can increase the players' focus, as well as add a degree of difficulty to the drill.

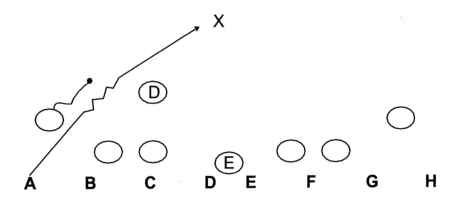

"A-H drill progression" — player D goes against the FB;
player E vs. the snapper.

Drill #73: SPIDER HANDS BLOCK DRILL

Objective: To teach punt rushers the proper angle and positioning of their hands at impact; develop focus and concentration on the block.

Equipment Needed: Several footballs.

Description: This exercise is very similar to the punt block on a mat drill (#70), but is done with an emphasis on hand positioning. This drill is more ideal for interior people. Players form a line five yards from the block point, looking at the side of the ball. The first player in the line extends his arms connecting his thumbs and index fingers, while spreading his fingers as far apart as possible. When the punter moves, the first player approaches block point and looks down through his hands as he blocks the punt. He then runs past the punter and attempts to catch or scoop up the blocked punt. The drill continues until all players have cycled through and successfully blocked a punt.

Coaching Points:

- As a rule, each coach has a preferential way of teaching hand positioning. This drill provides coaches with a rapid-fire way of repping a player's ideal hand positioning.

- This drill is most appropriate for interior players and their rush angles. It is designed to teach players to run through the punt with their hands leading the way and their eyes seeing the ball through their hands.

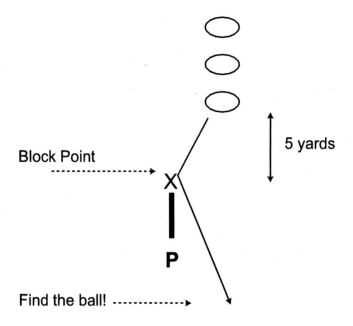

Drill #74: SCOOP AND SCORE DRILL

Objective: To develop a scoring mentality in a punt-rush unit; encourage players to smartly handle the ball following a blocked punt; increase hand-eye coordination.

Equipment Needed: A football.

Description: A scout punt unit is assembled in the formation that will likely be used by a team's opponent. The team runs its regular rush look against the scout unit. As the rush unit approaches the punter, the punter takes the ball and either rolls the ball behind or to a side, or throws a wounded duck pass over the line of scrimmage. The rush team players must first determine if returning the ball is in their best interest (i.e., did the ball cross the line?), or attempt to "scoop and score". The players must keep the ball in front of them at all times – as they scurry the ball downfield, players must communicate with each other to determine who is going for the ball. The drill is over when someone gains possession of the ball, when the ball goes out of bounds, or when the ball is fallen on in the end zone.

Coaching Points:

- This drill is a fun warm-up exercise. The players get an opportunity to push or knock the ball forward, while attempting to grab the ball. The coach should not be a negative reinforcement if the players cannot pick up the ball at first. The primary objective of the drill is to control the ball's momentum and keep it going toward the opponent's goal line.

- The coach should make sure to "throw in" some punts that go for positive yardage. This drill offers a great opportunity to work on team communication skills.

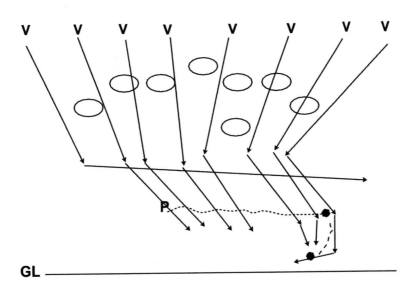

Drill #75: PIVOT, DROP AND BLOCK DRILL

Objective: To develop open-field blocking skills by teaching the punt return's stages of emphasis; enhance awareness in open space; teach good blocking angles; help limit penalties due to illegal blocks; develop return man's cut-back ability.

Equipment Needed: Dots or small cones; several footballs; a punter or a jugs machine.

Description: This is a partner drill. In this drill, four players line up on the line of scrimmage about 10 yards apart. Four other players (partners) line up 20 yards downfield to serve as coverage people (toward the return man). A return man awaits the punt at regular distance. On the snap, punt return men pivot their hips and drop off the line of scrimmage, glancing at the punter to check fake first. After they see the ball punted, each player will turn and drop to the return man. Upon being passed downfield by the return personnel dropping, the four downfield players cover the punt to the ball. Punt return players are to acquire their blocks after taking their angle to the punt, then occupy their men for two seconds. The ball is fielded by the return man and returned through the traffic until someone tags him.

Coaching Points:

- The following four-step progression should be taught: 1) drop off the line, 2) check the fake, 3) determine the ball's trajectory (i.e., find and listen to the return man), and 4) acquire and occupy target player.

- This drill is a great exercise for teams that run man or wall returns.

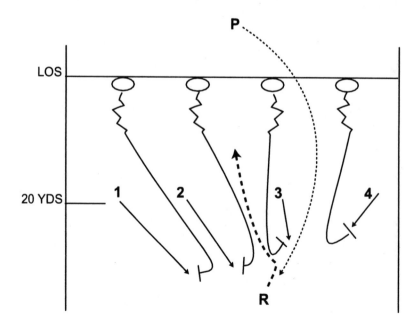

Drill #76: PULL 'EM, DRIVE 'EM, or HOLD 'EM UP DRILL

Objective: To develop superior hand techniques at the point of attack; increase balance and body control at the point of first contact; teach diversity in return techniques.

Equipment Needed: Six to eight shields (optional).

Description: In this drill, the first and second punt return teams partner up based on relative size. After dividing up, the players face each other across two lines with the punt return players all on one side. The players should give each other three yards of breathing room. Both players assume the appropriate stance (either punt return or punt). The coach then calls out a block he wants the return men to execute. He has three choices: pull, drive, or hold-up. After calling his command, the coach gives a directional call of right or left. Following the directional call, the coach says "ready" and blows a whistle. On the whistle, the players execute their technique upon impact with their partner. The drill should last for five seconds or until the technique of the return team players breaks down.

Coaching Points:

- The coach should work with his player's hand positioning. Properly conducted, this drill can be helpful in eliminating many holding penalties.

- Shields are optional. The punt team is just a show unit that offers minimal resistance. The shields may help provide the tone of this drill. If the coach wants to make it more difficult on the return team members, the punt team should be told that they are free to react. In that situation, the punt return team should be given that call in the huddle. To a degree, the drill then becomes similar to the 1-v-1 drill, but with a "stop coverage" emphasis.

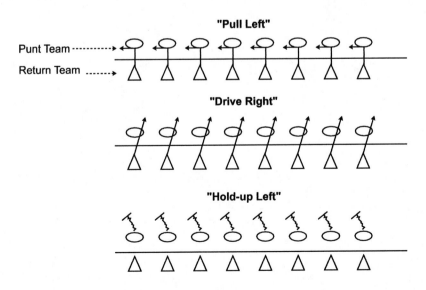

Drill #77: TWO-WAY WALL DRILL

Objective: To prepare players for running wall-based returns; teach locations in a wall punt return; condition the speed necessary to execute a successful punt return.

Equipment Needed: Eight or more dots, depending on how many men are in the wall; possibly a jugs machine.

Description: The field should be arranged with a return man deep (or however many return men are typically used) and the line of scrimmage as the drill's starting point. Dots should be placed beginning at 35 yards downfield and spaced five yards apart and two yards outside, as shown in the diagram below with four dots. A similar dot placement should then be done to mirror the opposite side of the field. On the snap, the players drive into the man in front of them, while counting to two-one-thousand. After the count, the players drop (from outside-in or inside-out depending on your scheme) and sprint to their landmark in the wall. When they reach their landmark, they adjust to the return man, taking the wall toward the ball. The return man can take the ball to either wall. With their heads on a swivel, the blockers shuffle, with the return man running behind them.

Coaching Points:

- Depending upon the scheme, either the outside rushers can fall out first, or the inside rushers.

- The drill can also be adapted to work both sides at pressuring the punt, and then walling to the opposite side of their pressure. The dots should be moved up five yards closer for the pressure wallers.

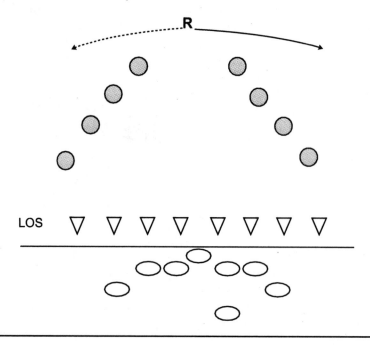

CHAPTER 7

KICKOFF DRILLS

Drill #78: HIT THE LINE SPRINTING DRILL

Objective: To develop timing in the initial phase of kick coverage; enhance acceleration on kickoff coverage.

Equipment Needed: A tee; a football.

Description: In this drill, the first and second kickoff teams fall in behind each other in their normal positions. A coach stands in the middle on the kicking-leg side of the tee on the line of scrimmage. The kicker takes his regular approach steps. On the kicker's or coach's command, the first group to the right side of the kicker approaches the line. Their objective is to be on or just behind the line as the kicker swings through the ball. After running through the line, the group runs 10 yards downfield before decelerating and returning to their line. After providing immediate feedback, the opposite group runs through the drill (the first group on the left side). The drill alternates until all players are consistently hitting the line of scrimmage at full speed, within a yard of the scrimmage line.

Coaching Points:

- If two different kickers are used in the drill, both kickoff team groups should be provided opportunities to work with each kicker. The timing involved in getting to the line is almost always different with each kicker.

- If the drill employs two coaches, they should stand on opposite sidelines, looking across the kicking line. They should note and record those players who have timing problems and work with them, individually if possible.

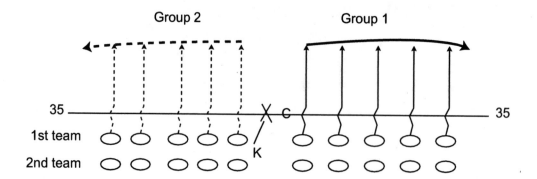

Drill #79: SCATTERED TIMING DRILL

Objective: To develop timing to the restraining line (i.e., the kickoff line); teach players deception in their run to the line; provide variety in working on line timing and kickoff coverage.

Equipment Needed: A football.

Description: The coach stacks up (placing two or more players together, one behind the other) his kickoff team. The right side should mirror the left side. The kicker takes his regular approach steps. On the kicker's or coach's command, the first group to the right side of the kicker approaches the line. Their object is to be on or just behind the line as the kicker swings through the ball. After running through the line, the group runs 10 yards downfield before decelerating and returning to their line. After providing immediate feedback, the opposite group runs through the drill (first group on the left side). The drill alternates until all players are consistently hitting the line at full speed and within a yard of the scrimmage line.

Coaching Points:

- For teams that like to add wrinkles to their start, this drill is ideal. It prepares players to hit their landmarks from a variety of starting points. It also teaches them to use their speed in the open field.

- With certain stacks, the kicker may have to delay a second or two after making his "ready" call to ensure that everyone in the stack can get to their locations. This is more true in 4- or 5-man stacks.

- You can be creative with this drill, or just run out of your game-day stack look.

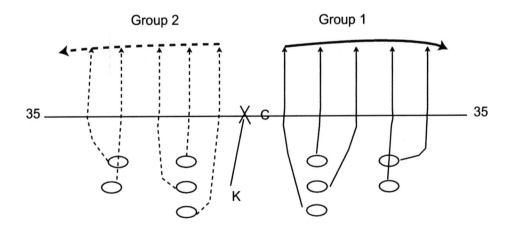

Drill #80: MULTIPLE SKILL HALF-LINE COVERAGE DRILL

Objective: To break down and work on the basic skills necessary for successful kick coverage; develop good decision-making skills; practice kickoff coverage at full-speed, while minimizing the potential for injury.

Equipment Needed: Five full-size dummies; a bag of footballs.

Description: The field is arranged, as illustrated in the diagram below. The first line of scout team players stands at the 40-yard line directly in front of one of the coverage lines. The second scout line stands at the 20-yard line, corresponding with a coverage line, but only three yards apart. The coverage lines then assemble for a half-field drill. (Note: The diagram shows the left side covering the kick while the right side players fall in behind their corresponding position.) The drill begins with the approach of the kicker and the coverage unit. The coverage personnel should run at full speed in the first segment of the drill. Upon reaching the first line of scout players, they must execute either a rip, swim, or 'run-and-recover' move without compromising their level of speed. They then recover to their coverage areas and continue to the next line. At the next line, the coverage people must take on and leverage the bag closest to them (i.e., disengage and corral the ball carrier). After the coach has released the first group of players, they get back into line.

Coaching Points:

*   If the team is short on scout team players, all the kickoff cover groups should simply be rotated into the two lines of return obstacles. Following each repetition of the drill, players should be bumped up from the end zone.

*   The return men should react to the drill side only (1/2 field). If the kick is not fieldable, another player or coach should be ready to toss a ball quickly to the return man. This procedure can save reps!!

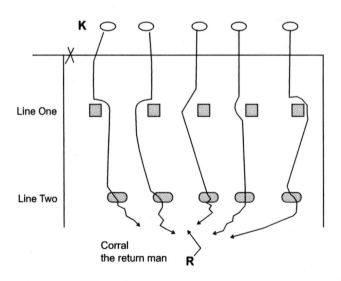

Drill #81: INTERCEPT DRILL (KO/KOR)

Objective: To warm-up; develop proper foot movement and body positioning for blocking and tackling in the open field; enhance coordination.

Equipment Needed: A pair of cones for each paired group.

Description: The players pair up and get into 5-10 groups depending on the number of players (each group should have two pairs). The cones are aligned three yards apart. One of the players (B) stands facing his partner one yard behind the cones with his hands behind his back. The partner (A) stands five yards in front of the cones, facing player B. On command ("hit" or "go"), player A runs toward player B, forcing B to intercept him. If B intercepts A effectively, A stops at the cones or puts his hands on B and tries to pull him out of the way. B must keep A in front of him at all times without using his hands. If B gets faked out or does not compensate with his feet, A can continue through the cones. Ideally, B should hold off A's attack for at least five seconds. To increase the difficulty of the drill for player B, the cones can be widened to 4-5 yards.

Coaching Points:

- When in a balanced intercept position, B must work his feet to gain the leverage advantage.

- Player B should use a visual cue and keep his eyes on the number of the attacker (A).

- Player B should maintain a firm, wide base underneath of him.

- Using quick, 'wiggle' coverage moves, the competitive nature of the drill should be emphasized to player A.

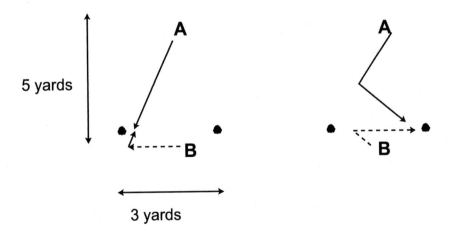

Drill #82: CRISS-CROSS COVERAGE DRILL

Objective: To develop kickoff coverage skills; improve execution of crossing in kick coverage; improve agility and open-field running skills.

Equipment Needed: A football; a tee.

Description: The kickoff team forms four lines behind its regular kickoff spots (i.e., 1's and 2's). In this drill, the coach commands his players to "criss-cross" (i.e., switch responsibilities immediately after the ball is kicked). The kicker then gives his ready signal, and the four players commanded approach the ball and hit the line at full speed. After covering 10 yards at full speed, the four players execute a switch stunt and adjust to the kick's location. The drill is completed when the four players involved in the drill reach the 35-yard line. As soon as the first group has been critiqued, the next four players in line go. After working the drill from a middle perspective (1's and 2's), the drill can be moved outside (2's and 3's), eventually working the kickoff team from all different perspectives.

Coaching Points:

- The primary emphasis of the drill should be placed on the players hitting the line full speed TOGETHER. The stunt will not work if one player is not running at full speed by the time he reaches the kicking line.

- Coaches should look for players who can keep their bodies under control, while executing the stunt and adjusting to the kick. Some players will take to this skill naturally and develop into players who can execute the skill in game conditions.

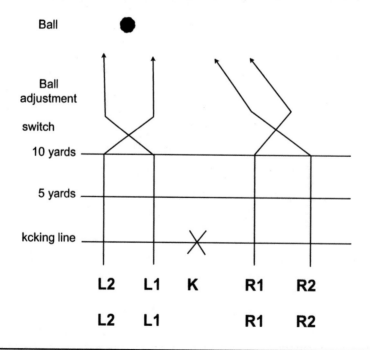

Drill #83: WEDGE ATTACK DRILL

Objective: To develop an understanding of how to stop a wedge return; develop the techniques necessary for defeating double-team blocks in the open field; teach the players their roles in stopping a wedge, while limiting dangerous contact in practice.

Equipment Needed: Five shields; a football.

Description: A wedge is assembled at the kick return's 20-yard line. Each person in the wedge is given a blocking shield. A return man is positioned 10 yards behind the wedge, holding onto the ball. The kickoff personnel are aligned three yards apart from each other, across the field at the return team's 35-yard line. The coach gets his players ready to work against the wedge by activating half of his kickoff team (e.g., the left side). He then tells his wedge which direction he wants them to go (e.g., to the right). On the "go" call, the kickoff team runs down the field closing on the wedge. When the coverage team reaches the 30-yard line, the wedge gets a "go" call from the return man and works the play. The coverage personnel selected must execute their wedge responsibility and shut down the running lanes to their side. Players can practice their 'attack-and-react' skills on the wedge.

Coaching Points:

- Complexity and/or difficulty can be added to the drill by incorporating variations to the drill, such as forcing four players to cover the wedge (pull one man out), or using players from both sides (i.e., L5, L4, L3, R1, R3 attack a middle wedge) to simulate players who have been blocked or who are not in good position to make the play.

- The coach's calls should be hidden from the coverage team so they have to read the apex of the wedge each time. For example, the wedge can be assembled on either hash mark and either sent at the coverage, or up the middle. The primary emphasis should be to play the wedge properly and to have the players see each other's roles in attacking the wedge.

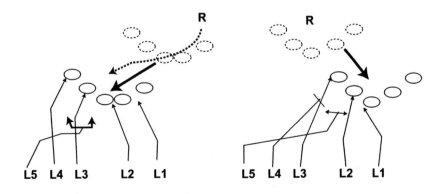

Drill #84: CROSS FACE DRILL

Objective: To teach players the importance of reading the body language of a blocker; improve reaction time to kick returns; develop good hand-eye coordination.

Equipment Needed: None.

Description: The players partner up and face each other five yards apart. One player is designated as the coverage player, while the other serves as the kick-return player. The kick-return player angles to one side (45 degrees). The coverage player then sprints at the blocker head on, and then executes a cross-face move on the blocker and adjusts his course to the return. The players then switch roles and continue working on the drill until each player has completed the drill five times.

Coaching Points:

- The importance of reading returns based on a blocker's body language should be emphasized. Mastering this skill can help players to be able to make the necessary adjustments 'on the fly' during games.

- Hand moves, like the rip, swim and club, are preferred, but quick speed bursts, strong running form, and butt-and-separation technique are also the necessary methods that coverage players can employ to cross face.

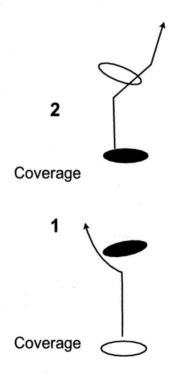

Drill #85: CONTAIN AND LEVERAGE DRILL

Objective: To teach outside skills against various returns; develop an understanding of contain and safety-role players and their relationship in coverage.

Equipment Needed: Two cones; a football.

Description: Two cones are placed at the 20-yard line, one on the sideline and one 15 yards inside. Two lines of outside leverage players are aligned at the 30-yard line in their respective positions, while two scout players line up on the near hash mark on the 15-yard line with a return man 10 yards behind them. The coach shows the scout team players one of three looks: double-team closest player; single kick-out both players; or log block the near player and kick-out the outside player. On the whistle, all players begin executing their assignments. The objective of the drill is to cover the kick properly and prevent the return man from getting into the speed alley. Players should work on utilizing their leverage skills and executing their assignments properly in order to ensure a well-run play.

Coaching Point:

- As the team gets more efficient in their outside coverage skills, the assignments of the outside players (safety – contain-to-contain – safety) can be switched. This step can provide each player with a more thorough understanding of both coverage responsibilities.

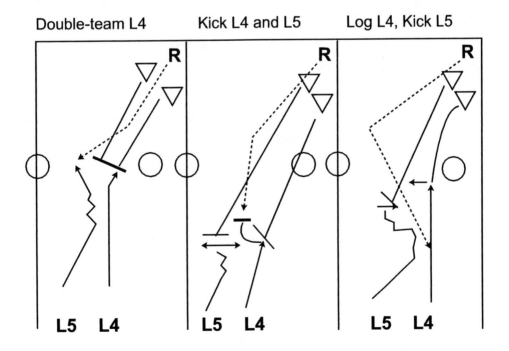

Double-team L4   Kick L4 and L5   Log L4, Kick L5

Drill #86: ENGAGE AND REACT DRILL

Objective: To develop quick reaction skills in the open field; use leverage skills in coming off blocks and tackling on kickoffs; teach good decision-making skills; provide an event in practice to effectively judge the speed of return men.

Equipment Needed: Six cones; a shield; a football.

Description: Four cones are placed in a square with approximately five-yard sides. One cone is positioned five yards upfield from the box in the middle, and one cone is set five yards downfield from the box in the middle. The backline players (i.e., the wedge players) and scout team people begin the drill from one of the extended cones, while the coverage players start from the opposite cone. The return man stands behind the backline player with a ball in his hand. The backline player should have a shield, unless the drill is done live (1-v-1). The drill begins with a whistle that is a signal for the two players to run at each other. The coverage player has to gain his balance and use his hands and leverage to defeat the blocker. After counting to two or three (depending on the drill's difficulty), the return man runs through the drill, trying to use his block to accelerate through the hole. It is the coverage man's responsibility to force the return man to stop his feet and make the tackle after leveraging the block.

Coaching Points:

- The difficulty of the drill can be increased by sending the return man on a two count. This step will give the coverage player less time to leverage and react. To start the drill, a 3 or 3 count works best for developing ideal coverage.

- The drill can be employed as a 1-v-1 drill to provide competition between backline players and interior coverage men. Often times, backline players are not involved in kick cover as starters.

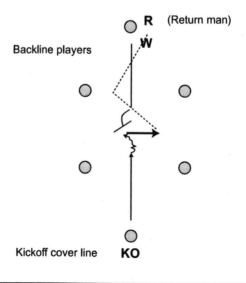

Drill #87: RUSS PURNELL'S* 'ROLL IT' COVERAGE DRILL

Objective: To improve team coverage and recognition of returns; develop an understanding of an opponent's return schemes; combine a walk-through coverage mode with quick repetitions; limit the amount of contact, while teaching coverage fundamentals and instruction.

Equipment Needed: A football.

Description: The drill is designed to break down coverage from the 50-yard line to the stopping of the ball. The coach assembles the scout team in a huddle and shows them a return card. The frontline stands on the 40-yard line, while the backline is aligned either at the 25-yard line or staggered somewhere in the approximate area. The return men stand at their regular depth. When the coach commands "roll it," the drill begins. The drill is conducted at about a 75% pace. The drill involves having the scout team go to their blocks and having the coverage unit recognize the return and react to stuff the play. The drill is completed when the ballcarrier has no room left to run. The ballcarrier can move slightly faster than 75% to force movement by the coverage unit. After the coach has completed his verbal cues and tips, the kick team recycles, and the return team gets another card to work.

Coaching Points:

- As many coaches as possible can be employed in the drill to critique the coverage unit. If a team has a limited number of staff, the drill can be conducted on one side at a time to ensure that each player has to go through his coverage thought process.

- This drill is ideal as the season goes on and the coverage team becomes more experienced because it saves the players' legs and bodies for game day, while working on the proper body positioning and mental habits of effective cover.

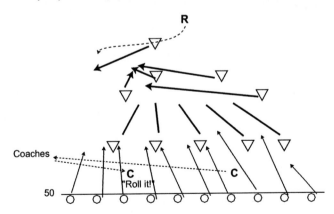

* Russ Purnell was the special teams coordinator for the
Super Bowl XXXV Chamion Baltimore Ravens.

CHAPTER 8

KICKOFF RETURN DRILLS

Drill #88: DROP ANGLE DRILL

Objective: To develop good habits and efficient steps on the kick return frontline; improve form blocking and footwork; develop good decision-making skills in blocks.

Equipment Needed: None.

Description: Five players (e.g., the first return team) assume a position across a line. The other five players (e.g., the second return team) are then aligned five yards in front of the return players with their backs to them. The coach then calls a return, either right or left. On the coach's command, the first player in the frontline group drops at his angle. When he passes the second-line player nearest him, the second-line player begins running downfield in coverage mode. The frontline player must confront his block, and either wall him off or take him across the field (against a cross-face, coverage move). The drill is completed when each player in the frontline has completed both right and left drops.

Coaching Points:

- The coach should go over the assignments with each individual player (e.g., who are you blocking? 'L4'). He should make sure that players drop at the appropriate angles on the front and backside of the play.

- The body position and foot and hand movement for each player should be critiqued. If running short on time, the coach should have the front side two and the backside three go in a basic return.

Coach: "Return right! Who do you have?"

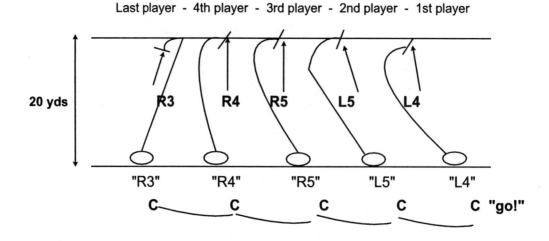

Last player - 4th player - 3rd player - 2nd player - 1st player

20 yds

R3   R4   R5   L5   L4

"R3"   "R4"   "R5"   "L5"   "L4"

C   C   C   C   C "go!"

Drill #89: DOUBLE TEAM DRILL

Objective: To develop good teamwork in a double-team block; ensure proper technique in a double-team block.

Equipment Needed: Cones.

Description: Two return players stand five yards apart on the goal line; the remaining return players stand in lines in the end zone. One line of coverage people is positioned on the 15-yard line. The coach tells the double-team which direction they are blocking (i.e., their post and lead assignments). On the whistle, the coverage man runs down the field. His job is to beat the double-team without running away from them. The post man on the double-team sets up in front of the coverage player. The lead man must mesh with the post man just after first contact. The double-team must either move the player well out of his lane or occupy him for at least five seconds to win the drill. The coverage man's goal is to get past the double-team and into the end zone. The drill is completed when one of the desired results is achieved.

Coaching Points:

- The players should be taught the two elements of the double team and the importance of both emphasized.

- If the coverage player crosses face and runs away from the double-team, the block becomes a one-on-one with the post man. The lead man trails, looking for either the most dangerous man to block, or the coverage man to cut back (refer to the diagram on the far right).

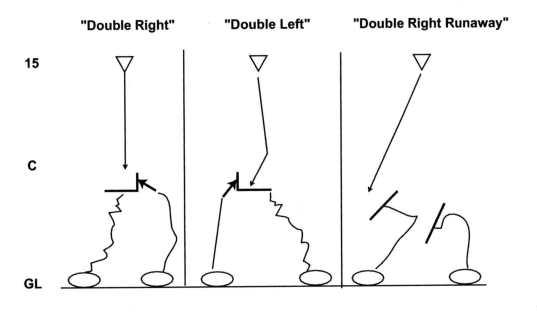

115

Drill #90: SHORT SET AND RUN DRILL

Objective: To teach the short-set frontline block and recovery; develop diversity in blocking techniques; develop hustle; enhance the concept of getting to a block.

Equipment Needed: A cone; a shield; a large bag.

Description: One player is given a shield and positioned at the 30-yard line. A second player takes a big bag and stands 40 yards from the shield holder. The frontline players get into a line at the restraining line (45-yard line). On the "go" signal, the player holding the shield simulates a coverage player who is running downfield. As the coverage player crosses the line, the first player in the line runs at him and executes a solid drive block, or a "crack-back" block, on the coverage player. On the coach's whistle, he then releases his block on the shield, locates the second target, and sprints to it. Upon reaching the second bag, the player must balance and drive through the bag using a wide base, with his hands inside. The player needs to take a good angle to set up the second block. As soon as the first bag holder resets, the next player in line goes. The bag holders need to recover quickly to keep the pace of the drill fast and furious. After working the short set to one side, the sides of both the blocks are switched (e.g., run the drill from the left side).

Coaching Points:

- If a frontline player is knocked down in a game or pancakes his man, the importance of recovering to another target and making a technically sound block should be emphasized.

- The coach should stress good footwork in the different blocks (e.g., "crack back" or short set block; the downfield scoop block).

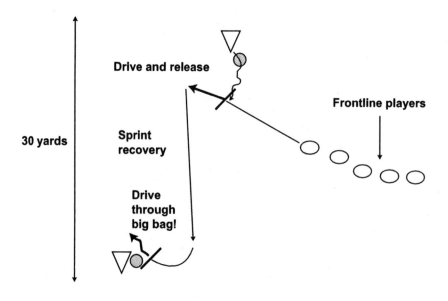

Drill #91: FRONTLINE DROP AND SWITCH 2-ON-2 DRILL

Objective: Improve communication on the backside of kick returns; develop proper body positioning in open-field blocks; prepare for teams that run switches or open-field stunts.

Equipment Needed: None.

Description: This drill is essentially a two-v-two exercise. The frontline kick return players are positioned in two lines at outside positions (e.g., guards and tackles) on one side of the field. Two lines of coverage players are then taken and located at kickoff starting positions that would correspond to the frontline player's blocking assignment. The coach tells the coverage players to either switch or cover normal. The kicker executes steps on air, and the drill begins. The frontline players must first determine if a switch is necessary. The call is made by the inside player. After his decision, the two players must use one of three different blocking techniques to block the coverage men: post block – keeping his body between his man and the side of the return; wash block – using his man's forward momentum to 'throw' him downfield out of control and behind the play; or ride block – if his man attempts to cross his face to get to the play, he must ride him across the field, while keeping his body locked up inside and lower than his opponent. After working on one side, the drill is then run on the other side.

Coaching Points:

- The call must be made from the man closest to the return to prevent a miscommunication.

- Using good base positioning and footwork for each block attempted should be emphasized.

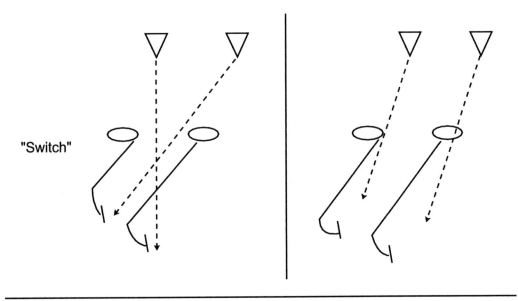

"Switch"

117

Drill #92: THINK FAST WEDGE IDENTIFICATION DRILL

Objective: To develop confidence and continuity in a back wedge; prepare wedge players for various game scenarios.

Equipment Needed: Shields.

Description: A back wedge with the proper amount of players for the designed scheme (this drill employs five players) is assembled. The wedge players group together and turn to face the near end zone (i.e., they face their own return man). The second wedge players are then assembled with shields at various locations in front of the wedge, but within 10 yards. The coach stands at the 10-yard line and gives a "go" call, while jogging toward the wedge. On the "go" call, the wedge quickly turns around together, and the shield carriers attack the wedge in various locations. The wedge people sort out the threats posed to them by the shield carriers and block them based on their assignments. The coach provides feedback from a return man's perspective and checks for holes in the wedge.

Coaching Points:

- The number of players who attack the wedge should be mixed. A minimum of three and a maximum of six (one too many) can be used to test how the blockers sort out the most dangerous players.

- If a man pick-up scheme is run with the wedge, this drill is good for preparing against teams that do a lot of stunting, crossing, or stacking to confuse the attacking team's count system.

5-v-5

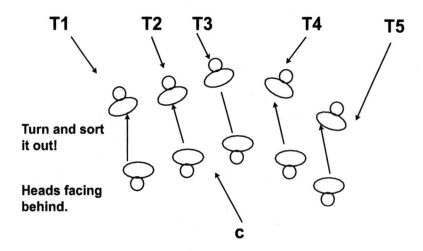

118

Drill #93: BACK WEDGE INSIDE-OUT BLOCKING DRILL

Objective: To develop continuity and good decision-making in back-wedge, double-team blocks.

Equipment Needed: None.

Description: A coverage player stands at the 35-yard line, and the back wedge is positioned in the middle of the field on the 20-yard line. A coach gives the coverage player one of three options: hard contain; jump inside; or sprint outside. On the "go" call, the wedge and coverage players begin moving. The back wedge must make the correct double team block, either a kick-out block with a good mesh point; log block with the inside man taking primary responsibility; or wheel block with the outside man taking primary responsibility. On the log and wheel blocks, the opposite player becomes free and turns to look inside for pursuit or immediate threats.

Coaching Points:

- Both the right and left sides can be worked with this drill.

- A coach can try all of his players in this decision-making drill in order to help determine who he wants in his back-wedge positions.

5-v-5

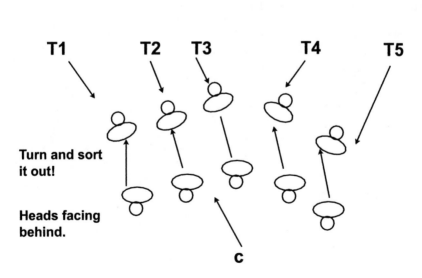

Drill #94: MIRROR DRILL – KR/PR

Objective: To warm-up; develop proper foot movement and body positioning for blocking and tackling in the open field; enhance coordination; recruit key muscle fibers for open-field play.

Equipment Needed: Cones or a marked field.

Description: The players pair up and get into 5-10 groups. Two cones are positioned three yards apart. One of the players (B) stands facing his partner one yard behind the cones with his hands behind his back. The partner, player A, stands one yard in front of the cones facing player B. On command, player A begins quick juke movements back and forth between the cones in an attempt to force B off balance. Player A can do any assortment of moves as long as he remains on his side of the cones. Player B must move his feet back and forth to counter A and maintain proper body position in front of A. On the whistle, B balances up, rolls his hips forward and coils his hands into A's number, using a wide base to drive block him five yards to complete the drill. The whistle can be randomly timed between 5-10 seconds from the start of the drill. The drill can be made into a tackling exercise by having 'B' wrap up 'A' instead of working his hands inside.

Coaching Points:

- It should be emphasized to the players to work hard to develop foot speed and quickness.

- The focus of player B's eyes should be maintained on the low number of his opponent. A common mistake of players in the open field is to focus too high or too low on their opponent's body.

- The player's hips should be maintained in a good explosive position, with proper posture. This emphasis will help ensure that the players will have a proper blocking base, while rolling their hips in the final phase of the drill.

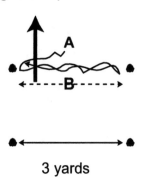

3 yards

C

Drill #95: HANDS TEAM ADJUSTMENT DRILL

Objective: To develop good communication and reaction skills of the kick return team to onside kicks.

Equipment Needed: A football.

Description: The hands team is assembled in their base alignment. Two kickers, one facing for a right side kick and the other for a left side kick, stand behind the ball. The coach makes a call to force the hands team to shift their alignment ("overload right", or "overload left, load outside"). The team must react to each call made by the coach. Then, on the coach's command, one of the kicker's fakes the kick, and the other kicks either an onside kick, a pop-up kick, or a deep kick. The hands team players must recover the ball. On the deep kick, the hands team players recover 5-10 yards and look for blocks.

Coaching Points:

- The coach can mix which kicker kicks and in which order to add variety to the drill. Continuously kick, recover and unbalance your hands team until you want to critique them.

- This drill is good for getting quality 'team' reps in a relatively short amount of time.

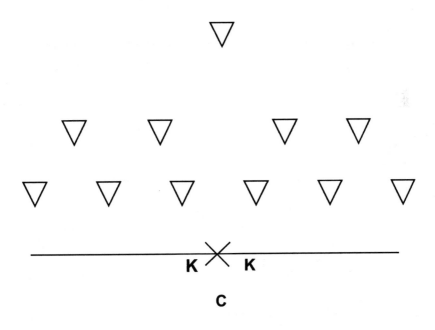

Drill #96: PEPPER KICKS DRILL

Objective: To prepare hands team players for fielding onside kicks.

Equipment Needed: A football; a kickoff tee.

Description: Two hands team players stand 12 yards from a kicker. The kicker tees up the football and practices different types of onside kicks, from high kangaroo kicks to low hard kicks that are directly at one of the hands team players. One of the two hands team players must correctly field the ball, while the other protects the area. After fielding four kicks from the right, the duo moves to the middle for four kicks and then to the left for four kicks, all-the-while gaining practice at handling kicks from various angles and positions.

Coaching Points:

- If a team has a converted soccer player as its kicker, the coach should have him kick a few left-footed (opposite his dominant leg) kicks. Players need to see a variety of kicks for the drill to be as effective as possible.

- If the hands team is organized by position, the players could be paired in a way that corresponds up to the hands team. Furthermore, the frontline players and the backline players could be mixed together, in addition to those who play side-by-side.

Players who are side-by-side:	Frontline and backline players mixed.

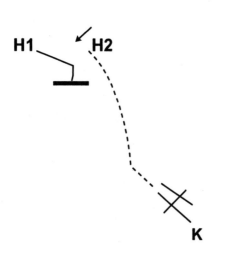 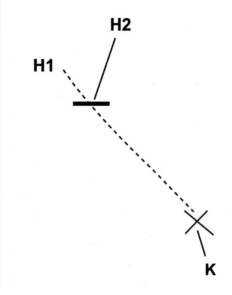

PART IV

COVERAGE AND
OPEN-FIELD DRILLS

CHAPTER 9

TACKLING & TURNOVER DRILLS

Drill #97: STRIP AND RECOVER DRILL

Objective: To develop an aggressive, turnover-based attitude; prepare players to create and recover fumbles.

Equipment Needed: Two footballs; four cones.

Description: Two cones are placed 20 yards apart. Behind one cone, two players — a ballcarrier (BC) and a stripper (S) — are positioned. Next to the other cone, a recoverer (R) stands. On the whistle, the ballcarrier runs toward the second cone. The stripper chases from behind to punch, hammer, or strip the ball free. The recoverer then scoops up the ball and runs to the first cone. The ballcarrier and stripper then switch roles and come back. After each has gone through the drill, a new group of three players execute the drill. Two groups engage in the drill simultaneously.

Coaching Point:

- The strip first (hammer down, punch out, or rip out) and then the scoop-and-score by the recoverer should be emphasized.

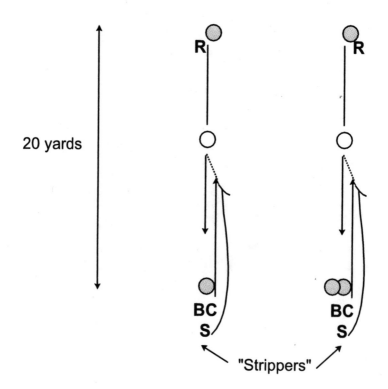

Drill #98: GRIP AND STRIP DRILL

Objective: To develop an aggressive, turnover-based attitude; prepare players to create and recover fumbles.

Equipment Needed: A football.

Description: A ballcarrier (BC), a tackler (T) and a stripper (S) stand approximately three yards apart. On the whistle, the tackler steps up to the ballcarrier and wraps him, while forcing the elbows of the ballcarrier up. The stripper jumps into the tackle and rips the ball free from the ballcarrier and then sprints away with the ball. The players switch roles until each player has gone through the progression at least twice.

Coaching Points:

- The tackler must raise the ballcarrier's ball-carrying elbow to help the stripper gain separation.

- The ballcarrier should hold on to the ball tightly in order to increase the difficulty of the drill.

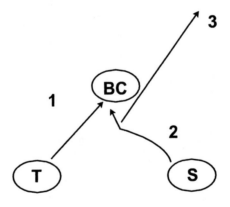

Drill #99: PURSUIT STRIP DRILL

Objective: To encourage an aggressive, turnover-seeking demeanor; develop good recovery strategies in coverage.

Equipment Needed: A football.

Description: A ballcarrier (BC) holds the football in his outside hand standing three yards in front of a pursuit player (S). On the "go" call, both players begin running. The ballcarrier allows himself to be caught from behind. The pursuit player reaches out and grabs the ballcarrier's off shoulder and pulls it back to slow the ballcarrier down. The pursuit player either executes an uppercut through the ball with his fist, or reaches over the top of the ballcarrier and hammers down on the ball. The pursuit player follows through on the tackle by wrapping up the ballcarrier.

Coaching Point:

- The coach should motivate his coverage players to play hard, even when they're trailing the return man. This situation often offers them the best chance to force a turnover.

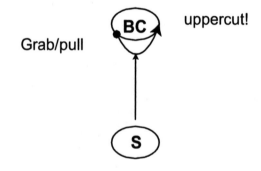

Drill #100: SEEK AND DESTROY OPEN-FIELD TACKLING DRILL

Objective: To teach and practice good form and balance when executing open-field tackles.

Equipment Needed: Fourteen dots; a football.

Description: Two rows of seven dots (one every two yards) are aligned 10 yards apart as shown in the diagram below. On one end between the two rows, a coverage man/defender (D) lies on his back. On the other end, a ballcarrier awaits the ball which is held by the coach. To begin the drill, the coach tosses the ball, simulating a kick or punt, to the ballcarrier, who then catches the ball and begins advancing toward the coverage player. Immediately prior to the ballcarrier making the catch, the coach calls "seek and destroy," signaling the coverage player to spring up and make the open-field tackle between the dots.

Coaching Point:

- The defender should be worked from a push-up position, simulating the experience of being knocked down. Often times, players who have been knocked around can re-acquire the ball and get in on the tackle.

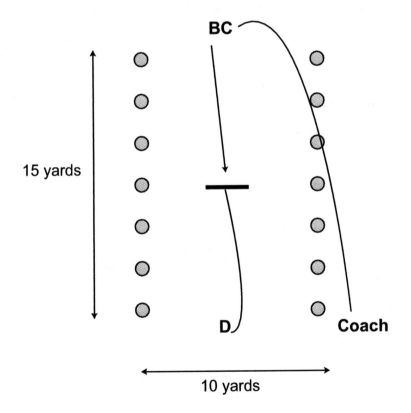

BC

15 yards

D

Coach

10 yards

Drill #101: TACKLING ALONG THE SIDELINE DRILL

Objective: To teach and practice good form and balance when executing sideline tackles; teach good use of the sideline as an extra tackler.

Equipment Needed: A football; seven dots.

Description: Seven dots are arranged in a row, spaced two yards apart and 10 yards from and parallel to the sideline. A ballcarrier stands to the inside of the gauntlet created between the dots and sideline. On the opposite side of the gauntlet stands the tackler (D). The drill begins by having the coach give a "go" call, which is a signal to both players to run into the gauntlet and compete. The objective of the tackler is to make the tackle and use the sideline as an extra tackler throughout the coverage. After making contact with the ballcarrier, the coverage player accelerates his feet and attempts to drive the ballcarrier out of bounds.

Coaching Points:

- To increase the level of difficulty of the drill, the drill could be either combined it with the open-field tackling drill or the cones could be positioned five yards further apart.

- This drill is very good for punters, kickers, and safety players.

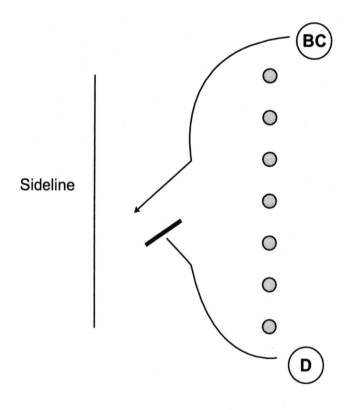

Sideline

Paul McCord is widely regarded as one of the most outstanding young special teams coaches in the game. Paul was a punter, kicker and quarterback at the University of Delaware and Western Maryland College. He earned GTE Academic All-America honors and was named all-Conference twice as a punter and kicker. McCord became the first Western Maryland graduate in over twenty years to sign an NFL contract when he signed with the Dallas Cowboys in 1995. In 1999, McCord was a player/coach in the Regional Football League, where he led the league in punting and was the only player in recent professional football history to snap, hold, kick, kickoff, and punt in a season. Shortly after the RFL season ended, McCord signed a contract with the Baltimore Ravens.

McCord got his start in coaching working at Mount Pleasant High School in 1994. Following his contract with the Cowboys in 1995, McCord began a six-year career at Western Maryland College as special teams, passing game and recruiting coordinator. The Green Terror led the nation in kickoff-return average in both 1997 and 2000 and punt return yardage in 1998. In addition, Western Maryland set 12 other school and conference special teams records under McCord's tutelage. The Green Terror held a regular season record of 39-1 over his final four seasons, winning four consecutive conference championships and qualifying for the NCAA national playoffs each year.

Perhaps his biggest break came when Raven's head coach Brian Billick offered McCord an opportunity to work with Russ Purnell and the Raven's special teams for the 2000 season. The Ravens won their first World Championship, while finishing fourth overall in NFL special teams play. McCord assisted with the punters and kickers, while working on computerized scouting and personnel breakdown and assisting Coach Purnell with game-day management and charting. In 2001, McCord served as special teams coordinator for Joe Gardi and the Hofstra University Pride in Hempstead, New York.

A defensive back, punter, kicker, and tight end in high school, Paul was the MVP of the 1989 Delaware Blue-Gold High School All-Star Game that is conducted annually to benefit the mentally handicapped children of the First State. To this day, Paul is an active alumnae of the game and a firm supporter of the mentally handicapped in Delaware.